ENDORS

MW00811549

Start your consulting business right, and the results will astound you: a sterling reputation, peak job satisfaction, and clients chasing you rather than vice versa. Start off on the wrong foot, and find yourself more stressed and discouraged than ever. Fortunately, we now have the combined wisdom from premier consultants Levine and Winiarski to make sure you design your consulting business from the ground up in ways that virtually guarantee success. Excellent!

Marshall Goldsmith – The Thinkers 50
#1 Leadership Thinker in the World

This practical book, based on years of experience, shows you how to become valuable to your clients, get greater results, and earn more money.

Brian Tracy, author - Now, Build a Great Business

A must-read book for business consultants! In one easy read, this book provides everything you need and more. *The Ultimate Game Plan* will become your go-to bible to get your business moving fast.

Teresa de Grosbois, President, Wildfire Workshops Inc.

Rarely do you find such gold within a single chapter, I dare you to get through the first one and not want to share with your friends. Great book!'

Greg S. Reid, Author - Think and Grow Rich series

As someone who already built a successful business and now working as a hybrid coach/consultant, I found this book invaluable. I had no idea all the ways I could impact my prospects and clients AND make money. Terri and Pete share so much value in this book, you would be doing yourself a disservice not buying it. You want results fast, this book will guide you to getting results fast. Buy it today!

Val Neighbors, Keynote Speaker,
Sales Strategist & Business Consultant

Many business books fall short. This one doesn't – in fact, this book provides everything you need and more. Way beyond expectations. For anyone who wants to accelerate their success and take their business into overdrive, get this book!

Lane Ethridge, founder Changing Lanes International

No stone is left unturned. As a veteran marketing consultant business improvement is a continual process. Winiarski and Levine have nailed it. This book not only gives the new business owner a solid foundation but, provides the reminders and nuances that seasoned consultants must implement for our businesses to thrive. Now I know exactly how to continue to elevate my business. "The Ultimate Game Plan – How to Power

Up Your Consulting Business and Skyrocket Your Revenue" is he go-to resource for all consultants.

Laura Rubinstein, Digital Media & Marketing Strategist, Transform Today. President, Social Buzz Club.

As an author, coach, and publisher I see many great books. The Ultimate Game Plan by Terri Levine and Pete Winiarski is outstanding... Get this book!

Keith Leon, Publisher, and creator of the YouSpeakIt Book Process

This book is a must read for all looking to grow their consulting business. It is written in uncommon common sense language that is simple to understand yet very powerful when applied. They speak from experience that lends total credibility to their advise. A handbook to be read more than once!

Helen Ober, Living the Empowered Life Business Coach/Consultant

I have been in the business of consulting since 1999. Initially as a management consultant within a boutique consulting firm, then since 2004 as an owner of a consultancy. I went through all the stages aptly described in the book, wow what an adventure it has been! I had an office of 8 consultants, I was a solo "star" and recently moved back to the US to re-start my consulting business in Boston MA. This book is a real gem, I wish I had it years ago as I was learning the hard way about the ins and outs. Terri Levine and Pete Winiarski describe everything you want to know about consulting and make it really easy to see how consulting can be a lucrative business opportunity. What's more they provide from the trenches know how and great ideas, information and inspiration! Thanks!

Michael Nir, CEO, Super Consulting, Inc.

From structuring your business and positioning yourself as an expert to must-have skills, the Ultimate Game Plan by Terri Levine and Pete Winiarski reveals the complete framework necessary to succeed in business consulting. A must-read!

Zaza Giroday, Chief Feminine Influencer at www.FeminineInfluencers.com

This book by Terri Levine and Pete Winiarski really hits the mark! They pull back the curtain so you can understand how consulting works and is full of ideas so you can add consulting to your business today.

Ben Gay III - The Closers - *www.bfg3.com*

Finally, a book that unveils all the secrets of becoming a leading business consultant. As a new business consultant, this book provided me with the "golden nuggets" I need to build and sustain a thriving consulting business. It talks about "being real" about what type of consulting business you are building and having laser focus on your Core Unique Positioning Statement (CUPS.) The importance of sticking with the vision for your consulting business adds so much value to me at this early stage in building my own consulting business.

Pete and Terri's book, "The Ultimate Game Plan" distills all the wisdom and steps you need to know and take to be a business leader and/or business consultant. Brilliant! Read it, follow the steps and watch the results. Replace your business library now with this one book that has most current and relevant business processes. It's the bible of business consulting!

Ilka V. Chavez, Corporate GOLD, LLC

Where was this book when I started consulting over 27 years ago??? The Ultimate Game Plan would have saved me years of having to 'figure it out'. No doubt that this should be required reading in business school. It's a must read for every serious business advisor and consultant. Apply these solid lessons fueled with your heart, intention and experience and create business results for all stakeholders.

David M. Corbin, author Illuminate *and Preventing BrandSlaughter - www.davidcorbin.com*

Terri and Pete's *The Ultimate Game Plan* condenses the real world work they teach in their Business Consultant Institute live trainings. Here is the proven combination of mindset and methodology I deployed as a participant (and so can you) to rapidly redefine, reinvent and ramp up my consultancy to higher levels. I was able to easily handle challenges, leverage opportunity, and incubate a new body of work with greater legacy impact. Now it's your turn. Grab this guide and put YOUR game plan in action.

Robert Merlin Davis, RobertMerlinDavis.com

Terri Levine and Pete Winiarski knock it out of the park! They share their best secrets so you can understand how consulting works and is full of ideas so you can add consulting to your business today. I wish I had this book back when I was getting started!

Seth Greene www.MarketDominationLLC.com

THE ULTIMATE GAME PLAN

Terri Levine & Pete Winiarski

M⊙tivational PRESS®
LEADERS IN GLOBAL PUBLISHING

Published by Motivational Press, Inc.
1777 Aurora Road
Melbourne, Florida, 32935
www.MotivationalPress.com

Copyright 2016 © by Terri Levine & Pete Winiarski

All Rights Reserved

No part of this book may be reproduced or transmitted in any form by any means: graphic, electronic, or mechanical, including photocopying, recording, taping or by any information storage or retrieval system without permission, in writing, from the authors, except for the inclusion of brief quotations in a review, article, book, or academic paper. The authors and publisher of this book and the associated materials have used their best efforts in preparing this material. The authors and publisher make no representations or warranties with respect to accuracy, applicability, fitness or completeness of the contents of this material. They disclaim any warranties expressed or implied, merchantability, or fitness for any particular purpose. The authors and publisher shall in no event be held liable for any loss or other damages, including but not limited to special, incidental, consequential, or other damages. If you have any questions or concerns, the advice of a competent professional should be sought.

Manufactured in the United States of America.

ISBN: 978-1-62865-345-8

CONTENTS

SECTION I
WHY CONSULTING ROCKS!

SECTION II
OPTIMIZE YOUR BUSINESS FOR MAXIMUM PROFIT

SECTION III
HOW TO POWER UP YOUR CONSULTING BUSINESS

SECTION IV
GET CLIENTS WITH THE PACK MODEL

SECTION V
DELIVERING AWESOME VALUE

SECTION VI
TYPICAL CLIENT PROBLEMS

SECTION VII
OTHER IMPORTANT QUESTIONS ANSWERED

SECTION VIII
YOUR NEXT ACTIONS

ACKNOWLEDGEMENTS

• • • • • • •

WE HAVE BEEN ACTIVE IN consulting roles for decades, and there are many people we want to acknowledge who helped us to shape the ideas and thoughts in this book. We are driven learners and wholeheartedly believe in gaining wisdom and new lessons from every interaction we have in our personal and professional lives. All the jobs and roles we've held during our careers as entrepreneurs, executives, and consultants have enabled us to interact with many important people who have influenced our thinking. There are many key people from our day-to-day interactions that immediately come to mind as shaping our thoughts around consulting—the function, the industry, and the principles of building a consulting business. We want to acknowledge you here.

Independently we have invested in many programs and have hired coaches and mentors through the years—all of whom have imparted their wisdom for us to digest and adopt into our personal styles and approaches with great impact. Along our journey we have been blessed with the sound advice of so many business mentors, including Jack Canfield, Joel Bauer, Dr. Joe Vitale, Dr. W. Edwards Deming, Justin Sachs, Bill Sterlie, Jim Bunch, and Frank Kern, among others.

There are many clients that we had over the course of our consulting careers that have impacted our lives and our consulting approaches. There are too many to list by name so rather, just know that if you have been a client of either one of us in the past then we appreciate you for trusting us to help your business. It was the interactions with you that helped us shape our advice in this book so that we can effectively teach other consultants the best ways to create high impact and deliver value to their clients, just as we have for you.

We are both active members of the Evolutionary Business Council, and it was through our association in the Evolutionary Business Council that we met and became friends. We are very grateful for Teresa de Grosbois for her creating the EBC and for surrounding herself with a group of amazing leaders that we have the opportunity to interact with regularly.

We launched the Business Consultant Institute (www.businessconsultantinstitute.com) with a series of live events called Power Up Your Consulting Business. As you might realize, there are a lot of logistics to manage and we had a great team of people to support us. Those who helped us market the events: Mary Stone, Teresa de Grosbois, Pam Bayne, Beverly Bergman, Daven Michaels, John Halpin, Faith Ellen Sacks-Hupfl, Lisa R Epstein-Sacks, Samy Zabarah, Ken Rochon, and Luke Charlton. Those who built our websites, and wrote copy for our sites and our emails: Pat Zickefoose, Andy O'Bryan, Robert Merlin Davis, Allen Wilterdink, and Josh Gindea. Our sponsors: Ken Courtright and Allen Wilterdink of The Income Store, Cindy Tyler of Vervante, Zac de Silva of AccMe, Eric Langley of Abeo, and Teresa de Grosbois of The Evolutionary Business Council. Those who provided on-site support: Mary Stone, Mo Bailey, Christina Rogers, Kelly Bluestein, Dion Ramos, Gary Stuart, Enna Nguyen Chiang, Teresa Huggins, and David Tweedt. Our guest speakers and contributors: Keith Leon, Forrest Willett, Gia Heller, John-Leslie

Brown, Alex Montoya, Dr. Andreas Boettcher, Bill Sterlie, Steven Rowell, Charmaine Hammond, Laura Rubinstein, Hawk Mikado, and David Boufford. Our video resources who are helping us create products to compliment the content we present in this book: Mark Fraunofer, Alex Watson, Jon Iannacone, R.J. Wallischek, and Mitch Visser. Nick Wins (Nicholas Winiarski) composed the music for our videos. Sandra Phifer who is an amazing photographer and shot our promo portraits. Also, Liz McNairney and Ellen Mordas handled hair and makeup, respectively.

Our publisher, Motivational Press, has a wonderful team of resources that have made this book come together with true professionalism. Justin Sachs, its CEO, has been a great advisor and mentor as we planned out the book's content and the strategies to build the Business Consultant Institute brand with this book. We are thrilled about this book's look and feel, from the outside cover to the inside formatting. Justin, in addition to guiding your team, thank you for your ideas that will help this book be seen by thousands of eyeballs.

Writing this book was no small task! Our original outline evolved and grew until we pushed to make our manuscript due date with a mad sprint. James Conley, Nasir Jamil Akhtar, Kelly Bluestein, Christina Rogers, Marie Winiarski, and Lisa Morin transcribed our various recordings from our videos, webinars, and live events to create raw material for us to add to our first draft. Kathy Sparrow masterfully poured through our content and helped us turn our concepts into a cohesive book. Robert Merlin Davis, thank you for your last minute reviews and feedback. If it were not for you all we would still be writing! Nasir Jamil Akhtar, you are with us every step of the way to keep us on top of all our endless tasks to make sure everything that needs to get done is completed. Thank you!

A special thanks to Jack Canfield. It is an honor to have your foreword set the pace for what we are achieving with this book. You are a great mentor and friend, and we deeply appreciate you.

We want to call attention to all our fantastic mastermind clients and recognize you here. Thank you for your trust and support as you implement our suggestions and achieve outstanding results. You have loaded us up with great stories to share, which proves what we teach actually works! Notable acknowledgement goes to: Helen Ober, Ilka Chavez, Lisa and Paul Morris, Norma Hollis, Joni Holeman, Maryanne Ross, Dr. Lisa Kaplowitz, Liz McNairney, Dave and Betsy Garrison, Robert Merlin Davis, David Tweedt, Val Neighbors, Katy Bray, Zeb Severson, and Kathy Sparrow. Keep on crushing it!

Our teams back at our other businesses who keep things rolling for us while we joined forces for the Business Consultant Institute are invaluable and deserve the highest possible thank you: David Tweedt, Christina Rogers, Kelly Bluestein, and James Conley.

Lastly, this book would not have been possible without the support of our loving family members who understood the value of this project and allowed us the time and space to create this work. Mark Levine—always supporting our business and giving us space to work in our home, in Mexico, and late into the night. Marie Winiarski—you held the Winiarski home together with love and patience. Nicholas and Nathan Winiarski—you watched dad work a lot of 7-day weeks to get his homework done and prove to you it's way better to get your homework done early.

Thank you everyone for your support!

~ Terri Levine and Pete Winiarski

FOREWORD

• • • • • • •

BY JACK CANFIELD

For more than 40 years, I have studied, applied, written about and shared the science of success with students all around the world. My best-selling book, *The Success Principles*, features many tremendous success stories by business leaders, athletes, entertainers, politicians, entrepreneurs and others. I also have many of the same groups of people participate in my seminars and attend events where I am the featured keynote speaker.

While countless numbers of these people I know have outstanding stories to tell, many of the successful business leaders have received coaching and consulting to help them define and implement strategies to help them achieve the results they seek for themselves and their companies. Success truly is a team sport, and there is no reason to try to go it alone when there are highly capable coaches and consultants who can give you guidance.

Whereas coaching is a powerful skill-set that can help business leaders to identify and break through their barriers, consulting goes further. Great consultants utilize coaching skills in their work to maximize their effectiveness for their clients, and also have permission from their clients to be rather directive to what they need to actually do.

Consultants are bona fide subject matter experts and develop personalized strategies for their clients that will speed them on their path to their goals. They train their clients in different principles and approaches so that they learn and embody new ways of thinking and new tactics. Consultants also act as a pair of hands to help implement their strategies, and are available to assist their clients to navigate the problems that inevitably arise as clients struggle to apply the consultant's principles and achieve their desired results.

Many company leaders eventually leave their jobs to become consultants, using the business expertise they have developed over their careers. In addition, consulting is an exciting role that many coaches, trainers, authors, and speakers who work with business leaders could choose to learn and play. But here's the catch—consulting is different than acting as an employee in your prior career, and it requires a different set of skills beyond coaching, training or speaking.

The good news is that this book, *The Ultimate Game Plan – Power Up Your Consulting Business and Skyrocket Your Revenue,* is exactly the resource you need to help guide you in building a thriving consulting business.

The authors are both highly sought-after consultants, with a wide spectrum of experience that ranges from supporting entrepreneurs with their start-up companies to working with international corporations with revenues in the billions of dollars.

Both have been executives in corporate America, and both have hugely prosperous consulting companies through which they have both created millions of dollars of value for their clients.

As a highly sought-after speaker and success coach, I have the opportunity to meet many business leaders and entrepreneurs around the globe, and the number of people who aspire to make significant contributions to the world continually impresses me. Terri Levine and Pete Winiarski, the authors of *The Ultimate Game Plan*, are two leaders who are making a huge difference through their consulting work, and now they want to help you do the same.

Terri Levine is the founder of the Heartrepreneur™ Movement and the best-selling author of *Turbocharge – How to Transform Your Business As A Heartrepreneur™*. Pete Winiarski is the best-selling author of *Act Now – A Daily Action Log for Achieving Your Goals in 90 Days*. Through their popular books and their powerful consulting both authors have proven that they genuinely care about helping people create and enjoy more prosperous businesses and lives.

And with their Business Consultant Institute, Terri and Pete have now combined their wisdom and experience to help people learn the ins and outs of successful business consulting, and now they are generously sharing the secrets of their success with you through this book. This book is definitely the place for you to start if you want to create a booming consulting business with exceptional revenues.

I suggest you read this book slowly, taking the time to think deeply about how you will implement each of the ideas and principles they share. As you gain insight on the optimum business model, your ideal consulting approach, and the marketing ideas that you want to put into practice, always remember that the real value will come from your putting each idea into action and thus make your booming consulting business a reality.

To your great success,

Jack Canfield

CEO of the Canfield Training Group and Coauthor of *The Success Principles: How to Get from Where You Are to Where You Want to Be*

INTRODUCTION

• • • • • • •

WE ARE SO *THRILLED* THAT you have this book in your hands. That means that you are ready to *crush it* as a consultant!

Whether you are already a business consultant or are just now getting started, you are in the right place at the right time. You see, companies are hiring consultants now more than ever, and if you can build a solid reputation and become known as *The Go-To* consulting resource in your area of expertise, then you will ride the wave big time!

We, as your authors, will take you on a journey where you can attract your perfect client, deliver for them way beyond their expectations, and enjoy a lucrative stream of revenue and cash flow so you can have a profitable business.

In this book, we will tell you some secrets about the consulting industry and how to build a highly recognized consulting business with a superior positive reputation. We will share some of our best marketing strategies so that clients will knock on your door, and you will never have to chase them. We will describe some of the important choices that you'll have to make over time as your consulting business matures, and help you optimize your consulting approach and model to maximize your revenue *and* your time off.

Before we get started, let us tell you who we are, why we wrote *The Ultimate Game Plan - Power Up Your Consulting Busi-*

ness and Skyrocket Your Revenue for you, and give you some pointers about how we recommend you read this book so that you can maximize its value.

HOW WE GOT STARTED IN CONSULTING

We want you to get to know us better. Maybe you have been on one of our webinars or have come to one of our live events. Maybe you are a client of ours at the Business Consultant Institute or a client of our own individual consulting companies. Perhaps, you know us from other networks. Maybe you have never met us and are picking up this book because a friend or colleague recommended it, or you were doing some research and discovered this as a resource. No matter what your path to this moment, we want you to consider this the beginning of a long relationship as you learn from us and implement our strategies. Let's begin with how we got started with our own consulting companies.

TERRI'S STORY

My career began as a speech-language pathologist. I started my own private practice and then successfully grew that business, discovering I was better at growing a business than I was at being a speech-language pathologist. I sold that business and started into home art show consulting and loved the consulting aspect, helping others grow their successful art businesses. I also founded and did the marketing for many other companies, and realized people were coming to me to have me help them in their businesses. I did that for many years: consulting, coaching, and mentoring businesses of all sizes. Then I decided I would work in corporate America.

After working there for five years as president of a national healthcare company, I became very disheartened with how business was done. I had owned my own businesses prior to this experience and knew I wanted to change how people were doing business. I left my job and began coaching and consulting, and because I am a natural marketer, I had thirty clients in thirty days and never looked back. Now, I do have to say, my father, my husband, and my entire family thought I was nuts for giving up my career and my solid high six-figure pay with stock options. Yet, I just knew, in my gut, consulting was what I was meant to be doing and I had found my "home."

I instantly attracted a corporate consulting gig for a few hundred thousand dollars and have now worked with over 5,000 clients in over 247 different industries. I've worked with companies as large as General Electric and as small as a start-up solo-preneur. I am blessed to be doing what I love, loving what I do, and making a large impact on business today.

Along the journey, I realized I wanted to share my expertise and help other business consultants create the businesses they desire and deserve, since I clearly know how to do this. I continue to do consulting work through my own consulting and coaching company, Heartrepreneur™ LLC, and love making an impact on businesses.

PETE'S STORY

My first exposure in consulting was when I was a senior in college, working as a consultant through the Industrial

Engineering department for a number of companies in Western Massachusetts. The University of Massachusetts had received a grant and was providing consulting services to those who applied to be part of this program. I was one of a handful of students who were training statistical quality control methods (using processes that were a number of years later named Six Sigma Methodologies) and providing consulting as we helped them implement these principles. I took tremendous delight in sharing what I had learned and had terrific personal satisfaction seeing how my help benefited these companies. I was hooked on the idea that I could make a difference.

I then enjoyed ten years at the Wiremold Company, now internationally recognized as one of the few complete business transformations that integrated Lean principles across all of its business functions. I had the privilege of acting as an internal consultant and process facilitator, where I interacted with the external consultants we hired from Japan to help us to implement Toyota Production System methodologies. Not only was I interacting with them to improve the operations, but I was frequently the one to take them out to dinner and learn from them in the evenings as well.

These early consulting experiences, combined with the management roles that I had, enabled me to be ready when I had the opportunity to join the prestigious strategy consulting firm, McKinsey & Company. McKinsey has excellent processes to train new consultants. I also benefited from ongoing feedback and guidance through my years of development while at the firm. I was there for five years, leading engagements as well as holding internal responsibilities to build our Strategy and Operations Excellence practice. After my five years at McKinsey, I joined The Danaher Corporation and experienced what it's like to be an executive and part of the senior leadership team.

My next move after leaving Danaher was to start my own consulting company, Win Enterprises, LLC. This was a logical step for me for a variety of reasons:

First, I had lots of consulting experience and was darn good at it. I related well to clients, had problem-solving acumen, and was able to help them achieve stellar results.

Next, and I'll be honest about this—I was no longer enjoying the roles in corporate America. I saw firsthand how the quest for the monthly and quarterly financial numbers actually broke apart solid operating systems, and this, in turn, eroded the ability to sustain long-term results. I became disenchanted and really didn't want to have accountability in a company where I did not own the full spectrum of responsibility. My goals and aspirations didn't align with the work I was doing, and it just wasn't fun for me any longer.

Eventually, there came a time when I could no longer ignore an inner desire to run my own consulting business. I had the entrepreneurial bug—and I really enjoyed helping people. I realized there are tons of business leaders who can benefit from what I've learned over the course of my career and continue to learn today as we work with new clients, new situations, and challenging problems. Having my own consulting firm also gives me some freedom to choose the clients and projects that are a good fit for me, the freedom to spend time with my family when I want to, and because consulting is a lucrative career, it also creates some financial freedom as the revenues come pouring in. All this combined made running my own consulting company a great career move for me. I have not looked back.

Combined, we have tons of individual experiences, helping various clients since 1998 that add up to a wealth of knowledge from our working with small businesses to international corporate giants. We have been inside the most prestigious consulting firms in the world and have worked alongside independent, solo consultants. We are also mentoring consultants and helping our mastermind members through their challenges as they look to expand and grow their revenue, create models that offer more personal freedom, add consulting services to their other businesses, transition from coaching to consulting, and to figure out the best way to launch and grow their consulting business. We are working with brand new consultants and seasoned professionals, and are thrilled at their results.

SO WHY WRITE THIS BOOK?

We have been asked numerous times why we decided to write this book together. We wrote *The Ultimate Game Plan - Power Up Your Consulting Business and Skyrocket Your Revenue* because both of us enjoy our consulting businesses, have been successful at our businesses, and have learned over time how to achieve really good results with our clients. Additionally, we have been mentoring other consultants in our mastermind program to either begin or seriously amp up their consulting businesses.

We also believe that now's the time—*yes, we're saying this again*—to become a consultant, to be a better consultant—and see your career soar.

While mentoring our clients in our mastermind group, we noticed they came to us struggling with some of the issues that we had managed to solve. Also at our live *Power Up Your Consulting Business* events (www.businessconsultantevent.com), many participants were already training, coaching, and speaking. Adding consulting to their bag of tricks just made great sense —and great dollars, too. Yet, we noticed that the people who wanted to enter the field of consulting did not have enough information or knowledge to do so.

It also occurred to us that many questions were coming from consultants who are already successful, are curious about our successes, and wanted to know the shortcuts and secrets we possess as highly successful business consultants. These questions include: How do you do what you do? How did you start your consulting business? How should I set my fees? Where do I find more clients?

Being asked these questions again and again at our *Power Up Your Consulting Business* events, we had a light bulb moment. We realized the information we know and the systems and processes that we have set up can actually help a lot of people. That led us to summarizing the basics of building a consulting business, and it is why we decided to write this book for you.

Launching a consulting business can be broken down into five steps:

1. Declare your expertise and position yourself to the market

2. Develop the consulting skills to maximize value for your clients

3. Study the business of consulting and maximize your revenue and profit

4. Build a client funnel and master the art of getting new engagements

5. Grow your *revenue* and *build* your business

Many consultants focus on Step 2 and work to become a solid consultant who can deliver great value to their clients. The problem is that they struggle to get clients because they don't do Step 1, or later Step 4. Step 3 is critical if you want to maximize your financial position (and of course you do!). And, unless all you care about is your current status today, you will want to work on building your business over time, as in Step 5.

We are going to cover all of these topics within the pages of this book. We're not saying that it's not going to take some work. The good news is that in this book we paved the way for you to have a smoother journey.

WHAT'S IN THIS BOOK FOR YOU

We decided to take you behind the scenes and show you what works really well in our businesses so that you could get the kind of results that we are getting. By reading this book, we know you will gain the confidence and structure that you need to get started in your consulting business if you are new to this field. If you are already consulting, you will take your business to the next level. We want you to be hugely successful, with a steady flow of client work, doing the kinds of consulting you desire with your ideal clients. We also want you to have the tools and systems in place so that the consulting work you do with clients makes a big impact on them as well. Our desire is to help you create a massively successful consulting business. We know that when you do consulting the right way, with a high level of integrity, and can move the needle for a lot of businesses that are struggling, you will prosper.

Additionally, we feel strongly that business leaders do not need to struggle and that companies can run better and smoother. We want to ensure that business leaders know they can find business consultants with the right skill sets, right motivation, and high value to deliver great results. If you want to be one of those consultants, this is the book for you.

It has been a very interesting process writing this book together. As owners of two very successful consulting businesses over decades, and our past backgrounds that included a great deal of corporate work, we were able to merge the best of what Terri has learned, with what Pete has learned. Combined, we have worked with companies with as much as $80 billion in revenue and as small as $1 million in revenue. We knew that by sharing our systematized and automated processes, our frameworks, and our experiences you could synthesize them and quickly start or grow your business in consulting—and ultimately, have a great impact on the people and companies that you work with.

As you read the book, we encourage you to do something that you may not normally do while reading most books. We actually ask you to write in the book. Many believe you should never take a pen to a book. However, we believe that is hogwash. Research proves that engaging in a conversation with what you are reading will help you build a greater understanding of the material—and create meaning that is relevant to you. As you join the conversation with us, by making notes in the margin, writing down your questions, and highlighting sections, do whatever allows you to feel as if you're sitting across the conference room table from us.

So grab a pen or pencil and write notes in the margins. Fold pages over that you want to refer back to. It is okay. We give you full permission. Circle, underline, or highlight. Do whatever it is you need to do to retain the information from this book. Then you can come back to the strategies, techniques, tools, or lessons that will guide you most in your business. Our goal is that you get maximum value from this book and see it as a reference tool, to pick up and revisit anytime.

We consider this book a consultant's business and marketing bible. You do not have to reread the entire book when you want to refresh a memory. You can go back to a page that you folded or noted and instantly get the information you need. Just as your business is a dynamic resource, this book is as well. *The Ultimate Game Plan - Power Up Your Consulting Business and Skyrocket Your Revenue* will help you through the challenges you have as you're starting and growing your consulting business.

And along with the contents of this book, you'll have access to bonus resources, such as videos and sample documents, on our website.

www.TheUltimateGamePlanBook.com/resources

SECTION I

• • • • • • •

WHY CONSULTING ROCKS!

This section is here to get you excited about your consulting business. The industry is growing, and you have chosen to jump in and be part of it—or are considering making the leap. We want you to understand that now is the best time for you to go all-in, to build your consulting business with expectations of high revenues and fast results. You can become super successful and build the lifestyle and income level you dream of.

We also share some basic facts about consulting so we can be grounded with a common understanding of what consulting is, why clients want your help, and who is jumping into consulting now. We conducted a survey of current consultants, new consultants, and also potential clients, and we think you'll find that you are just like the other people who are on this journey, too.

Are you ready to get started? Turn the page...

CHAPTER 1

· · · · · · ·

NOW IS THE TIME FOR YOU TO GROW YOUR CONSULTING BUSINESS

IF YOU'VE EVER THOUGHT of becoming a consultant—*now* is the time! It's an industry that's growing at a phenomenal rate. Tons of companies are looking for help to turn around their company, solve challenging problems, or take the business to the next level.

According to *Forbes,* the business consulting industry is a $100 billion per year industry. This is larger than the Internet marketing industry that weighs in at only a $19 billion a year. Also, the business consulting industry is said to be experiencing massive growth. In fact, business consulting has doubled in size over the last few years, and it is expected to double again by the year 2018.

Think of your favorite example of a tremendously successful industry that expanded very quickly and made all the companies in that industry super successful at the same time. Imagine if you were able to jump on the Internet bandwagon and be one of the first household name websites. Now, that's what we're talking about, but without the bubble to burst because businesses will *always* need assistance to achieve the ever increasing expectations they have on their shoulders to be faster, more productive, super efficient, and make a greater impact on the market. You can help them get the results they seek and enjoy a steady stream of clients and increasing fees as you go!

SO WHO COULD CONSIDER CONSULTING?

Business owners, authors, trainers, speakers, business leaders, coaches, specialists, and experts...to name a few.

Virtually anyone who has expertise or skill set that would help someone achieve their business goals, or goals as a business leader or manager (including personal goals), can be a consultant. In fact, we're willing to bet that you may already be a consultant and not even realize it.

* If you have "how-to" expertise, products, or services...

* If you have a business where you show your customers how they can get the most from your products or services...

* If anyone has ever asked your advice...

Then you are a consultant—and you are leaving money on the table by not acting and promoting yourself as one.

THE SURVEY—CONSULTANTS ARE JUST LIKE YOU

We conducted a survey of our mastermind clients and the people who have attended our live training workshop, *Power Up Your Consulting Business,* to find out about their motivations, their experience, and their aspirations to be consultants. Here are some of the insights we've gleaned from their feedback and from reviewing demographics, their motivations, and their aspirations.

DEMOGRAPHICS

* ✸ 90.4% of our survey participants were at least forty years old, which implies they have years of practical experiences that they have developed into expertise

* ✸ 65.5% have hired a consultant in their career, which means they have an idea of what interacting with consultants looks like and have some familiarity with the role

* ✸ 67.3% have worked as a consultant before, which also means that nearly one-third do not have consulting experience and are just starting their journey

* ✸ 34.6% have been consulting for longer than ten years and 15.4% between five and ten years, so there was significant experience in our survey participants

* ✸ 51.9% of consultants are women as compared to 48.1% men—implying that this is no longer a male-dominated industry

And we're guessing that you are probably not that different from other people who are now pursuing consulting.

MOTIVATION

* ✸ 96.2% want more personal freedom

* ✸ 46.1% are frustrated with their career

* ✸ 52.8% say that they have great expertise at something, and that people often ask them for help

Notice if people are asking you for your help on something related to their business. That is the market talking—potential clients are suggesting that you consult to them.

Consulting has the potential to be significantly rewarding and provide freedom and flexibility, so it's not surprising that the participants include these motivations that led them into the field.

ASPIRATIONS

* ✱ 86.5% have revenue goals for their consulting business
* ✱ Of those with revenue goals, only 15.6% are meeting their goals
* ✱ Interestingly, 51.9% do not have a strategy to achieve their goals

The point we want to make is that you (the reader) are just like these people who are already consulting or are pursuing consulting. There is no reason for you to not pursue consulting. So go ahead and acknowledge the fears and considerations that are rolling around your mind saying, "Yeah, but..." "I'm not like them..." "It's too risky." You may think that is the voice of reason, but it is the same voice that has kept you playing it safe for most of your life. We know. We've had many conversations with this voice—and we silenced it. The result—our highly successful consulting businesses!

GET READY TO EXPLODE YOUR BUSINESS

With this book as a resource, you will tremendously increase your chances of knocking it out of the park.

Consultants who operate an optimum consulting model are credible experts, who understand the business of consulting, and know how to save their client's money, deliver higher value—

and receive high fees as a result. Consultants earn 500% more money than any other start-up businesses, including Internet marketers.

Surely, if you are so inclined, you could capture some of that market share readily available for consultants. And we're ready to show you how.

**Remember, for bonus resources
related to this chapter, go to:**

www.TheUltimateGamePlanBook.com/resources

CHAPTER 2

• • • • • • •

LET'S FORM A COMMON UNDERSTANDING OF BUSINESS CONSULTING

To UNDERSTAND THE FUNCTION of consulting, we must first define the concept. Consulting is using your expertise, knowledge, and abilities to provide solutions to troubling challenges for a client, and having the client invest for your advice and services. You are being paid to provide an external point of view when you are a business consultant. Most clients also want you to raise the bar and give them extra motivation to achieve their business goals.

A business consultant provides an analysis of the existing practices of a company and makes recommendations for improvements. Some business consultants specialize in one area of business, such as supply chain management. Additionally, consultants can be hired to develop employee-training programs or to streamline operations. Many consultants have industry expertise such as retail, financial services, consumer packaged goods, or pulp and paper, for example. Consultants could have deep technical expertise such as engineering depth, IT programming languages, the ins and outs of social media like Facebook and the Facebook algorithms, website design, search engine optimization and Google algorithms, or maybe expertise about a certain type of equipment. There's also the consultants who have had a long career building upon their successes over and over again, have now retired, and are entering the consulting world where they help clients by sharing the advice based on their experiences and successes. The possibilities are almost endless.

Business consultants look at organizations and companies and begin consulting projects by understanding what clients wish to improve or fix. Typically, consultants first assess the situation the company is currently in by reviewing financial statements, evaluating competitors, and analyzing business practices. After the research phase is complete, then business consultants frequently develop a new business model and prepare recommendations and present them to the client.

Some business consultants have an undergraduate degree in business management or business administration, while others may come from backgrounds in marketing or accounting. Others understand accounting and management principles, financial models, marketing, and communications. And while some business consultants hold a Master of Business Administration (MBA), this is not necessary. Many come into the field with years of experience, and possess another type of degree, such as engineering, or perhaps none at all. It might surprise you to learn that quite a number of lawyers graduate with their law degree (JD) and join the big, strategy consulting firms like McKinsey and Company. They fit in well because they are smart, analytic problem solvers with great communication skills, two of the most important consulting skills as you'll learn in Chapter 11.

Now is a great time to be a business consultant because the field is set to increase by about 19% between 2012 and 2022. You must be thrilled that you're a consultant at this point in time because you can expect to see your business grow and rise along with the whole industry. And, while you apply the strategies we describe in this book, you will differentiate your consulting company enough to stand out as one of the best, so that if the industry ever does experience contraction, you'll be a thriving survivor.

Think of when there are real estate booms. Everyone in the industry booms too and makes tons of money—real estate agents, mortgage brokers, appraisers, etc. But as soon as the real estate bubbles burst, only the best of the best survive.

We will teach you to capitalize on the boom now while it's happening, and then be one of the best of the best so that no matter what the economy does, you will continue to thrive and enjoy revenue growth and a well-balanced lifestyle.

A QUICK INDUSTRY PERSPECTIVE

The consulting industry is tried and true and dates back to 1886, when the first consulting firm—Arthur D. Little, Inc.—was founded. The largest and most prestigious strategy consulting firms that cater to the Fortune 100 companies include the "Big Three": McKinsey and Company, Boston Consulting Group, and Bain and Company. Accenture is also another well-known large firm. The larger firms generally consider projects with clients who can afford their fees, which often are more than seven figures for each project and tend to generate follow-on projects for years.

In 1980 there were just five firms with greater than 1000 employees. By the end of the next decade, there were more than thirty firms with greater than 1000 employees. Plus, consider all the smaller firms with fewer than 1000 employees and the plethora of entrepreneur consultants—which may be you!

A business consultant works with clients on strategy, planning, problem solving, and the development of business skills and knowledge. As a business consultant, you may be doing anything from designing a business model or marketing plan, to determining which marketing techniques to use and how to use them, to defining your client's strategy, teaching and facilitating process improvement in operations, developing leadership skills, shifting the company's culture, or improving employee engagement. You may be helping your clients plan and implement projects, and you will always be called upon to give advice, teach skills, and brainstorm with your clients to produce practical results and enhance strategic thinking.

WHY BUSINESS CONSULTING?

You may wonder why companies continue to invest in business consulting even when there is an economic downturn and be surprised that the business consulting industry continues to grow by leaps and bounds. The reason is business consulting is responsible for keeping companies solvent and is why companies are growing even during the economic downturn. Many companies have only been able to remain in business because they engaged a business consultant.

There are a number of interesting dynamics going on in the business consulting industry. Today, there are a few giant consulting companies that are known as the largest strategy-consulting firms. These firms tend to work with large consulting teams and Fortune 500 companies as their clients. Then there are a number of smaller companies that do not have the same level of reputation as large ones, yet have similar approaches with a support model that includes multiple people on the consulting team helping to solve client problems in engagements that might last one to three months or longer. There are also a number of boutique firms that may have as few as ten consultants on staff or as many as a couple of hundred consultants. The boutique firms are much smaller than those larger companies that may have thousands of consulting employees and support staff. Boutique firms have started to grow in quantity over the years and through their experienced consultants, they reach a global market and have solid consulting client bases.

Lastly, there are the super small companies, many of which are one-person consulting companies. These one-person consulting companies launch when an individual decides it is time to hang out their own shingle and become a consultant. The business owner of these consulting companies may have the motivation to head in this direction because of the passion that individual feels for helping companies improve, or they may start their own business consulting company because they have already been a business consultant either in their previous career responsibilities, or they were an employee of a consulting company. They may have decided that they have had enough with their corporate America career and now they are ready to move on and do what they know best in a consulting role rather than as an employee.

One advantage of offering business consulting services is that you do not have to sell the consulting monthly as business coaches typically do. Business consulting can be sold on a project basis. Business consulting is a great business choice because you can set up your business to have a very low overhead without a lot of employees or without a lot of fixed cost. You can also establish recurring income. You can build your consulting business very quickly as long as you have "how-to" skills to help businesses.

Today, clients are ripe for business consulting services. With some focused marketing efforts, you can quickly find clients and you do not have to establish complex sales funnels—nor do you have to develop many products. You also are not required to spend a lot of marketing dollars. You can create a business that can be freedom-based with high net profits and lots of time off.

To find clients, you do not need to have expensive pamphlets or brochures these days. You can do very efficient marketing on the Internet, using tools like PowerPoint, Skype, GoToMeeting, or webinars. All of these tools allow you to sell business consulting at a much lower cost than twenty years ago or so.

One of the key ways to sell business consulting is by building a ladder of desire. You build a ladder by segmenting your ideal target audience and speaking to the exact people that you know have the problems that you are solving through your business consulting services. Once you really understand your target audience's key problems and their issues, all you really need to do is to demonstrate how you can solve their problems. Provide evidence that you have the answers to their issues by creating content that helps them solve their problems and shows your expertise.

Business consulting is very enticing to small, medium, and large organizations when you demonstrate to the leaders of these companies that you can bring them the help they want—and need—to achieve greater profits, revenues, business growth, business success, or whatever else they desire. It is very exciting for a business to look at bringing on a business consultant when a company sees that the consultant and their skills will result in more profits and a high return on investment for the organization.

Consulting today is much more sellable because companies are looking for higher profits and seeking tools that will make them more profitable. Most executives are reading articles in magazines like *Fast Company* or *Inc.* that point to business consulting as one of the things that will make their companies more profitable.

If you are considering becoming a business consultant, know that you are entering a profitable industry and a business that is also very sellable. Consulting allows you to enter the market quickly, and if you do a good job for clients, they will stay with you long term. Business consultants can build stable and steady incomes and have recurring income as long as they continuously do a good job for their clients. We will teach you in other chapters of this book how to do just that. We will also prove that clients are plentiful—if you follow a marketing system that works because there are a lot of companies seeking business consultants.

Once you identify a target market that is specific, and a target market you truly understand, you can continuously have an edge in that market. For example, if you want to be a productivity consultant, you become a known expert in that field. The same applies if you decide to be a sales consultant or an IT consultant. Whatever your niche is, become an expert in that particular area and you will succeed as a business consultant. And we will model how you can highlight your expertise.

Business consulting is a profession that can yield very high profits if you understand how to market your business and how to keep the business running with low overhead. Business consulting is basically selling consulting services that are "how-to" services. (In comparison, business coaching is typically based on helping clients discover their own answers.) We believe that when you combine "how-to" services with client discovery you will be most successful for the client and therefore have a highly successful consulting business.

With all of this in mind, if you are thinking about being a business consultant, realize you have a few simple options. Decide now if you want to be an employee in a consulting company or if you want to set up your own consulting business and then act as a contractor to other consulting companies, or if you want to have your very own consulting clients. Which one of these is calling to you? Would you prefer having built-in clients? If so, contract yourself out to other consulting companies. If you want something a bit more challenging yet more lucrative, then set up your own consulting company and go get your own clients.

Many business consultants do not necessarily have offices, and a great number choose to work virtually. Pick whatever model works for you. You might decide to have an office or to work from home. You might want to hire a lot of employees, you might want to only have independent contractors, or you might want to simply do all the consulting yourself. When you become a business consultant, you determine the path that is right for you. We help you understand these options more deeply in the next section. Read on and decide which model is best for you.

Ready to build or expand your consulting business? Then let us move on to the next section!

**Remember, for bonus resources
related to this chapter, go to:**

www.TheUltimateGamePlanBook.com/resources

SECTION II

• • • • • • •

OPTIMIZE YOUR BUSINESS FOR MAXIMUM PROFIT

In this section, we will review some key decisions you have to make about your consulting company and how you choose to do business. You have to make some choices about your business model. You will determine which of your areas of expertise will enable you to differentiate and establish a long queue of clients who want to hire you. You also want to consider which approach you will use in the different situations.

The good news is that none of these decisions are etched in stone. You can change your mind, and in fact, probably will make some changes as your business expands and/or matures.

CHAPTER 3

• • • • • • •

YOUR CHOICES TO OPTIMIZE YOUR BUSINESS MODEL

FUNDAMENTALLY, THERE ARE FOUR TYPES of business models to consider as you launch your consulting work. They are to be:

* an employee of a consulting company
* a contractor to other consulting companies
* a solopreneur consulting company
* a consulting company with employees or contractors

Let's look at each of these options and discuss the pros and cons.

MODEL 1: EMPLOYEE OF A CONSULTING COMPANY

A quick way to gain some consulting experience is for you to get hired by a consulting company. Most of the larger consulting companies have industry-leading training programs and opportunities to help consultants develop their skills and become highly effective consultants very quickly.

Of course, if you are entrepreneurial and are excited to launch your own business, then working as an employee in a large consulting firm may not be for you. While it might be a great first step to launch your career and speed up your learning curve, if you have genuine entrepreneurial aspirations, the prospect of you moving up the ranks in a company to become a partner may not be as inspiring as the idea of launching your own company. However, the good news about being part of another consulting company is that you have a steady paycheck and do not have the burden of finding your own clients.

Note: As an employee of another consulting company, you also do not need to form your own business. The advice and guidance given in Chapter 19 are for you to consider when you are ready to go out on your own, but not needed as long as you are an employee.

MODEL 2: CONTRACTOR TO OTHER CONSULTING COMPANIES

As a contractor to other consulting companies, you are not an employee of their company. You are your own company and can choose with whom you want to work. The strategy for you is to form relationships with multiple consulting companies who have more work than they can handle with their own employee resources. You, as a free agent, can decide if you want to agree to their offer to work on a project or not.

The advantage to being a contractor is that you choose when you want to work and with whom versus as an employee where you have to accept the assignments that are given to you. Your revenue is likely higher as a contractor than your salary as an employee. However, you might find long stretches of time when you do not have any contract work and are therefore earning no revenue.

MODEL 3: SOLOPRENEUR CONSULTING COMPANY

As your own consulting company, you need to find your own clients. This is exciting because you are fully functioning as your own decision maker as you grow your business. Your fee level is higher than you received as a contractor because there is no "middle person" who is taking their fair share. But, you have full responsibility for all the marketing, contracting, and executing required to find clients. You risk struggling to nail down client engagements at the frequency that you want to keep your business moving forward. The reward is a fee that could be 2-3 times or more than what you earned as a contractor.

As your own company, you must consider all the advice in this chapter. You will be at tremendous risk if you do not bother to choose your business structure and file the required forms. If you find yourself in this situation, schedule appointments with your CPA and attorney immediately!

MODEL 4: CONSULTING COMPANY WITH EMPLOYEES OR CONTRACTORS

This is where things really get exciting! Not only are you a consulting company that has more work than you can handle by yourself, you are also now enjoying the benefits of leveraging other resources.

Of course, with adding resources to your team you have other management decisions to make, such as hiring consultants onto payroll or building relationships with contractors. While an employee's salary will be a fraction of what a contractor would be when expressed as a per diem rate, you are responsible for getting your employees' utilization up to levels where they are paying for themselves and making you money. A contractor, on the other hand, is a truly variable resource that you can assign to a project or not.

You will also have other administrative responsibilities that increase as you add more clients and team members. If you spend your time on these tasks then, as Michael Gerber, author of *The E-Myth Revisited: Why Most Small Businesses Don't Work and What to Do About It,* says, you are not working *on* the business, but *in* the business. This is a dangerous place to be as a business owner. Your role is to create more revenue opportunities and not do administrative tasks just to keep costs down. Don't fall into this trap!

Clearly, as a consulting company with employees and contractors, you need to have the right business systems in place. It is also vital to have your business structure selected. By now that is obvious. You also must have well-designed contracts so your contractors (and employees) are clear as to what to expect from you and what they get in exchange. There are other elements such as confidentiality and non-disclosure agreements (NDAs) that you must have in place to protect you, your clients, and your resources. We discuss this more in Chapter 18.

Business systems are critical at this point, too. Creating proposals and client contracts are best designed when they are quick and painless. Your invoicing process and systems to manage cash flow will keep your resources happy and not leave you to seek other work.

YOUR INCOME OPPORTUNITY

Of course, with each of the different models you will have different risk/reward factors, and with the higher risk, your reward of enormous revenues can be quite lucrative. Let's review these factors and talk about the associated income opportunities.

MODEL 1: EMPLOYEE OF A CONSULTING COMPANY

In Model 1, you have no entrepreneurial risk at all because you are an employee within a consulting company. Of course, like all companies these days, you have to pick an employer that provides great opportunities for you to be challenged, allows you to develop as a consultant, business leader, and person, and one where you will enjoy working for years to come. You have the same pressures and expectations as employees all around the world, which include performing well and pleasing your boss so that you will get an admirable performance appraisal with a nice bonus and 4% bump in your salary.

As an employee, you have a salary you can count on. You get a regular paycheck that is predictable, and the only real question you have is how big your bonus will be each year. You can count on your financial situation to be stable and to grow slightly over time. You can plan to take a percent of each paycheck and contribute to your 401(k) plan, set more aside in your personal savings accounts, and use the rest for paying your bills.

So how much can you expect to earn? Remember that the median salary for 2015 was about $88,000, even though there is a range from about $65k to $140k. Choose the firm wisely and be impressive during your interview, and maybe you'll be lucky and end up on the higher end of the scale. Then, as you continue to perform well that number will go up, and maybe you'll get promoted to manager.

Now realize, the consulting firm is billing you out at some fee level, and then assigning you to a project team on a specific client. The majority of that fee is going back to the firm, with you collecting about 10-15% or maybe 20% of that fee as part of your salary and bonus. To put numbers to this, if your firm bills the client $2,000 per day for your time, you might collect $200-300 of that in your salary, earning you $1,000 to $1,500 per week or an equivalent of $52,000 to $78,000 per year. The reason the percent may be higher is that you will *not* actually be billable for fifty-two weeks a year. Naturally, you will enjoy a few weeks of vacation, attend training and company meetings, and have possible time between client projects where you contribute to non-billable work.

Notice these numbers are a bit lower than the median salary we shared above, so the firm is more likely billing you out more than $2,000 per day and the percent of your fee that the firm gives to you could be as high as 25%. In fact, for the range of $65,000 to $140,000 per year, your daily billing rate to the client might be $2,500 on the low side, or $5,000 to over $8,000 on the high side at the more prestigious firms, which is what would be required to cover for your non-billable time through the year. These are totally in line with the range of billing rates we are familiar with seeing, and depending on the firm have seen well above $2,500 or even $5,000 for consulting resources, and then highly tenured consultants in the more prestigious firms billing 2-3 times that level. Now *that's* something to aspire to achieve!

Don't get hung up on the exact number. The important thing here is to appreciate the order of magnitude. Your employer needs to pay a number of expenses just to have you on payroll, including your health benefits, a match on your retirement plan, and certain taxes. In addition, they need to cover all the firm expenses, including overhead and salaries for the more senior people, all from a percent of the fees they collect for having you at the client site. This doesn't leave you with a huge net percent of what you're billed out at, but then again you just have to show up. Your firm does all the work to find clients and manage the details.

MODEL 2: CONTRACTOR TO OTHER CONSULTING COMPANIES

As a contractor to the consulting company, you are not an employee. That means they do not have any responsibility to you for insurance benefits, retirement account contributions, bonus pay, vacation, taxes, or any of the other expenses that they would for their employees.

While a consultant as an employee is a fixed cost to the company, as a contractor you are a variable cost. According to your contract, if you do billable work, you get paid. If not, you don't. It's that simple.

You can expect a higher percent of the amount the consulting firm bills to the client to come back to you in the form of your fee, in the range of 25-50%. Now, usually there is no discussion about the actual fee to the client, but, instead, you negotiate a rate with the consulting company that is acceptable for the work that they are contracting you to do.

This means for the same illustrative $2,000 per day to the client, you would expect to invoice the consulting firm between $500 to $1,000 per day. If they were billing you out at $3,500 per day, you might expect $875 to $1,750, and if they were billing you out at $5,000 per day, then you would expect $1,250 to $2,500 per day.

Of course, you have to cover your own business expenses and cover your own health insurance, taxes, etc. so your actual net will be less. This is why you set yourself up as a business and make sure you have a proper accounting of your revenues and expenses. You're no longer thinking about your "wages," but now you have to think like a business owner in terms of your profit and cash flow.

For example, if you are happy earning a fee of $1,200 per day and can get that much from a consulting firm that hires you for a project at one of their clients, then congratulations! You have a successful project. The important thing to remember is that you being happy with your fee is independent of the fee that the consulting firm bills to their client for your services. In fact, you might never know that number. The consulting firm will decide to contract with you if they feel happy about the margin they make after they pay you for your services. It doesn't matter if they bill the client $2,250 or $4,250 for your services. If you're happy with $1,200 per day, then it's a huge win-win!

The numbers here are directional and meant to help you appreciate the differences across the different consulting models. Rather than get hung up on the examples, consider what per day fee would make you happy.

MODEL 3: SOLOPRENEUR CONSULTING COMPANY

In this model, you are your own one-person consulting company and have your own clients. The good news is that 100% of the consulting fee that you charge the client comes back to you in the form of revenue. That's very good news.

The bad news is that you are now responsible for everything to do with finding clients and securing contracts to keep you engaged. That can be a trick to do when you're on a paid consulting project, so what often happens is you have a client's project end and then there's nothing next up on the schedule—you have "feast or famine" revenue coming in each week or month.

Your reward for taking on the added risk and responsibility is the higher percent of fees that you end up bringing into your business, and you get to set the fees! This is where solo consulting companies sometimes have an advantage over the bigger firms, because they can accept a lower fee without the overhead that the larger firms need cover. With that said, the larger firms also have a greater resource pool to support the client and this might become important to your clients if they decide that you don't have the bandwidth to fully support them.

MODEL 4: CONSULTING COMPANY WITH EMPLOYEES OR CONTRACTORS

This is the maximum income scenario for you, because not only do you collect 100% of the fee to clients, but you now have other consultants on your team as employees or contractors. That means that you are also collecting a percentage of what you're billing for them to the client (50-90%, depending on the various factors we described above).

This is a more complex business model that means you will need some basic infrastructure in place to manage the resources, invoice clients, and pay your team's wages if they are employees or pay their invoices if they are contractors.

The absolute best news for you is that if you have a team of resources fully trained and indoctrinated in your methods and approaches, then you can work with more than one client concurrently. This is where your growth can *really* take off!

Now that you have an idea of the different business models and the income possibilities, take a moment to digest what seems like the best model for you given your experience and resources today. Have you already played the role of an employee (Model 1), and are you now ready to create your own business? Are you going to jump into Model 4 straight away or will doing so drown you?

The reality is that a blend of these models might make sense and will likely change over time. Take a look at this story to see what we mean.

THE EVOLUTION OF OUR CONSULTING COMPANIES

Let us illustrate some of these decisions with a story about how Pete added employees and resources over time. Here's Pete telling the story:

Early in my consulting business, I was a one-person company that did everything including the delivery of the work and all administrative tasks. I was talking to potential clients and writing the proposals, flew to client locations to lead the projects and deliver the work, and then created invoices and managed the other office functions. I had a *lot* of tasks to stay on top of, especially when I had more than one client.

Then there was the game-changing realization—I left the important task of sending an invoice to a client (so that they can write a check and pay me for the work I had done!) on my "to-do" list for well over a week. This is opposite of the advice I give clients, yet I was not managing my cash flow very well.

That's why I hired my first employee. She was with me for a few hours per week, just to start helping me clear the administrative tasks off my list more quickly. My cash cycle became a lot shorter as I would get invoices created and out almost immediately. This also meant that I had someone to follow up in ways I didn't when I was alone.

I had similar experiences when I began pulling contractors in to assist me with my clients. At first, I would have a second person join me on a client project so the client could get to know both of us. After a while, I would feel comfortable stepping away and letting the contractor deliver the work without me there. This created a ton of freedom and leverage for me as I could then build the next client or choose to have some downtime with my family. This ensured my sanity as my work/life balance was becoming very unbalanced. Delegating was worth every penny.

Another growth element of this story is when I hired my first full-time consulting resource onto payroll. I had two client proposals that both looked like highly probable seven-figure deals that would each require at least two to three resources. Hiring an employee rather than relying purely on contractors would be a no brainer, right?

Well guess what...exactly zero of these two contracts were signed for a variety of reasons. The dynamics inside the corporate world are very unpredictable. In one case, their revenue was dropping, and they suddenly had to cut back on the cost and discretionary spending. This meant some of the work they had planned for could not be funded so consulting got crossed off the list. In the other, the client decided that they would attempt to drive the improvement projects without any external support. (I later learned they did get some of the projected improvements, just not as much or as quick as they would have with consulting support.)

I now had an employee who had just started with me, all excited to launch into a long-term consulting assignment. I had to share the news that not only did we not get those two new clients, but I was instantly in a cash flow crunch and was going to have a tough time meeting payroll a month out. That is a scary conversation, to be sure.

The good news is I stayed committed, that employee stayed committed, and we weathered that storm. I now had a second person on my team to help with the full court press for business development to land new client work. We followed through on every lead that we had as quickly as we could. Now, some years later, that employee is the president of my consulting company.

From Pete's story, we can see that there is a huge reward from sticking with your vision for your company. Pete could have easily retreated and stayed a one-person company as a way to keep costs down, but that would have prevented the opportunity for significant growth.

You can also see that multiple business models can be part of your plan. You might realize that you can experience a lot of flexibility by contracting yourself to others (Model 2) while you opportunistically search for your own clients. When you land your clients, you can either do the work yourself or bring in a contractor to do the work on your behalf (Model 4). When that project ends, if you want to support your next client by yourself (Model 3) or announce that you're available to contract to others (Model 2), you have that flexibility.

Terri's story is different, and she shares it here:

I established my business and thought it would just be me doing the consulting work. Quickly, I saw that I could not handle all aspects of the larger consulting contracts that were coming in, and I needed to have additional help and people on my team who had expertise in areas that I was not as strong in. Initially, I took on a business partner, and then, quickly realized, for me, having a partner and not being the sole decision maker didn't resonate for me.

Once we dissolved our partnership, I hired independent contractors in many specialized areas of consulting to work on my team and with my company. I sought projects that would fit their expertise, and I was able to take on a lot more projects when I had a group of consultants ready to work. Over time, I was able to grow the company large scale, and we were involved in many projects across the globe. I, however, did not like managing so many consulting gigs and felt that I only wanted a handful of consultants in my company versus the large number we had grown to. I felt I could assure greater quality, value, and service, if I had fewer people working with my company. This past year, I scaled down the size of our consulting team, and only have a handful of the highest-level consultants I could find, all independent contractors, and we only do the work we are perfectly skilled at and matched for. By doing this, we get rave reviews, testimonials, case studies and the business has become a "by referral" business. This really works for me.

So as you can see, Pete and Terri demonstrated through their different journeys and experiences, as a consultant you get to select your business model and can change that model over time.

The next decision for you to make is to decide which areas of expertise you will declare as your focus for your consulting company. Let's dive into that next.

**Remember, for bonus resources
related to this chapter, go to:**

www.TheUltimateGamePlanBook.com/resources

CHAPTER 4

• • • • • • •

DECLARING YOUR EXPERTISE

EVERY CONSULTANT HAS ONE OR more specific topic areas they declare as their expertise. It's totally okay if you have a bunch, but be careful about having so many that you lack focus in your business or confuse your potential clients.

Imagine that everyone on the planet knows exactly who you are and what you are an expert in, and what problem you solve for companies. Anyone who has that specific problem would know that you and your consulting company are the person to contact.

That is the idea behind declaring your area of expertise. You want to create demand out in the marketplace for your specific types of projects.

The other thing about declaring your expertise is that you will become more of that expert. You will invest more time in studying the different challenges that clients have in your area of expertise, go out of your way to solicit client work in this area, and then by default have a larger volume of this type of project that deepens your experience. With this experience, you now have more practical examples from which to draw as you then write blogs and articles, get speaking engagements, and perhaps even write a book or two. All these lead to clients identifying with you as the expert even further. It is a very fortunate cycle for you.

A FRAMEWORK FOR SELECTING YOUR EXPERTISE

Generally, you can be known as an expert in a specific industry, in a functional area, or in specific processes. You can also have multiple areas of expertise in each and have that expertise spread across each. Let's discuss each possibility:

INDUSTRY

To become a known expert in an industry, it helps to have real experience in that industry. Maybe you had a twenty-year career in automotive, or pulp and paper, or in retail. Or, if you have had numerous consulting clients in a particular industry, you will end up learning the details of that industry. For example, Terri lives in the Philadelphia metro area, which is home to many pharmaceutical companies and has had a lot of pharma clients over her career so she can declare pharma as an industry that she specializes in.

FUNCTION

Think of the different functions within a business—marketing, sales, operations, customer service, finance, engineering, etc. Each of these functions also has sub-functions. For example, engineering might include product design, manufacturing engineering, research and development, testing, etc. Marketing could include marketing communications, market research,

Internet marketing, social media marketing, product development, etc. Operations could include supply chain, purchasing, receiving, capacity planning, scheduling, manufacturing, distribution, shipping, etc. We could go on and on, but you get the picture.

What of these areas do you have deep expertise? Maybe you started your career as an engineer supporting new product development and then shifted to create fixtures for new product production. Then, finally, you were a manufacturing engineer before you became a production manager. You might have some unique perspectives about product design, especially as it pertains to designing products to take manufacturing cost out of the product because you had this responsibility through your career and were quite good at it.

Some consulting firms specialize in one function, and become known as an engineering consulting company, for example. Other firms have a more broad perspective, but have consultants on staff who are deep experts in, say, market research.

PROCESS

Process expertise means that you know how something works. For example, facilitation skills lead to the process expertise of facilitating project teams. There are many consultants who are highly skilled at facilitating *kaizen* events, which is a process of implementing Lean principles and solving problems in a very focused effort over a duration of just a few days.

People who are process experts know a specific methodology to achieving some goal. They have run this methodology tons of times before and can do it in their sleep. The industry or function doesn't really matter. As long as the basic tenets of the process are in place, it's just a matter of applying the principles to the particular situation. For example, consultants who facilitate *kaizen* events may have their experience in automotive manufacturing, but then apply the same methodology to an underwriting process in an insurance company or any other functional area in any other industry.

Think of a unique way where you have managed to drive tremendous improvement in some business processes in the past. How did you do it? Can you make that method proprietary so that the way you do it is unlike how other people might do it? Can you call it some really cool name that you become known for?

SOME EXPERTISE EXAMPLES

When Pete was at McKinsey and Company, he had a number of retail client projects. This started because he had functional expertise in supply chain and specifically distribution centers, and he was responsible for distribution for a while when he was at Wiremold. In addition to the client work that included distribution, he was the author of a number of internal documents about distribution centers, especially applying Lean principles to distribution chains as well as the role of the distribution chain and the supply chain in a full Lean enterprise. Pete was one of the lead presenters at an internal company supply chain training, which further established him as an expert in this area. In fact, for years after he left the firm, McKinsey consultants would call him for advice on their specific distribution and supply chain projects. It's easy to see how you can become known as an expert in an area.

In another example, when Pete was a one-person company, he had grown tired of being asked to simply facilitate *kaizen* events for clients. He wanted to play at a more strategic level.

With some experience with *hoshin kanri,* a process for ensuring the company's strategic goals had the right focus and priority across the company to ensure the goals are met, he declared himself an expert in this area. He began writing articles and speaking on the topic, and soon became an external advisor to George Group, a medium consulting company, where he taught the principles to their consultants and advised their clients. This gave him more live case studies and experience to write more articles. The pinnacle of declaring this expertise is when the corporate strategy team of a $26 billion company called Pete, after reading one of his articles in *Industry Week,* asking for his help to understand how they can implement that process in their company. Declaring yourself as an expert works to attract clients who need help in that specific area to you.

Terri started out helping companies with marketing, sales, and leadership consulting, which she was already a known expert in, as that was her role in corporate America. She had been doing keynotes and writing papers and articles during her stint in the field of rehabilitation medicine. As Terri began writing books and speaking on stages in her own consulting business, she realized the market was calling upon her for her soft-leadership and people-development skills. Being a Master Coach and a Clinical Psychologist specializing in organizational behavior, Terri soon recognized that the market was choosing her. She shifted the focus of her firm to provide the market with what they saw her as an expert in, and her business grew rapidly.

A QUICK EXERCISE

If you're not sure what the best areas of expertise are for you, go through this quick exercise. Start by noticing what questions other people ask you about. Where do they ask for help? What type of help is it? What areas? That will give you a clue.

Next, what areas do you absolutely know you're proficient in? Where are you clearly one of the best around?

Lastly, what do you absolutely love? Or, if you're indifferent, what do you know you don't like at all?

Take the results from these three lists and prioritize the areas where you have people asking for help, where you know you're really a star, and where you are going to continue to love doing that type of work. As soon as you declare these areas, you will have clients signing up to do a lot of projects with you, so you'd better not hate that type of project or else you will begin disliking consulting!

GETTING RICH IN YOUR NICHE...REQUIRES A NICHE!

Here's where things could get super exciting for you. What if you specialized in a specific industry and were *the* go-to consultant for specific functional areas within that industry? *And* you had some proprietary processes that helped you make significant improvement and deliver huge value in ways that nobody else could do? Can you see how once the word got out you would become the absolute owner of that space?

For example, Joe Polish had a struggling carpet cleaning business in the early 1990s. Then he cracked the code and his business exploded. With what he had figured out, he began teaching other carpet cleaning companies how to market themselves and grow their businesses. Imagine that niche—teaching marketing to carpet cleaners. Today, Polish, who founded the

Genius Network, advises the likes of Sir Richard Branson, Body for Life's Bill Phillips, Tim Ferriss, and others. Now that's the intersection between an industry and a function—which leads to great success.

Terri is a Guerrilla Marketing expert and has written multiple books about this subject, including one for spas and one for beauty salons. This is a process expertise applied to two different industries. And, clearly she continues to incorporate Guerrilla Marketing techniques to help other companies, too.

Pete's company has a lot of experience in operations and strategy execution, and has some proprietary tools to help clients with business transformation. The intersection of function and process expertise! Starting to get it?

Now let's help you make some choices about your approach. Flip to the next chapter.

Remember, for bonus resources
related to this chapter, go to:

www.TheUltimateGamePlanBook.com/resources

CHAPTER 5

• • • • • • •

YOUR APPROACH TO CLIENT ENGAGEMENTS

CLIENTS AND CONSULTANTS ENTER INTO many different types of engagements. Clients could hire you for a number of sessions, days, or weeks, or they might bring you in every week for nine straight months. You may be hired to assess specific problems and determine their needs to crack the problem. They might ask you to help them create a new strategy and then support implementing that strategy. They could ask you to design and implement a specific project. Clients sometimes bring consultants on board to supplement their staff for short periods while they crack a specific problem or are recruiting a key resource.

Think about what kind of consulting approach you want to do. You might want to build your consulting company as the go-to company for leadership assessment work or some other type of business assessment work. You also need to decide if you want to swing for all big, long-term projects, knowing there will be gaps in between. Or, perhaps you would rather work with multiple clients simultaneously each month.

Consider also if you want to work with senior management teams on their biggest strategic problems, or if you want to work lower in the organization to help managers and their teams execute projects and solutions. Some people who are great working with senior leaders do not relate well with people at the line level, and some who are fantastic project execution people cannot hold a cohesive discussion with an executive. Recognize your skills and where you want to play as a consultant.

THREE BASIC APPROACHES

There are also different approaches to the consultant role and how you will interact with your clients. These are: Advisor, Done with You, Done for You.

The **Advisor** is one who shares expertise or tells clients what to do; he/she then leaves it to the clients to then implement strategies.

Using the **Done with You** model, clients get results because of your involvement in the engagement process; it possesses a training element where you teach the client and the client's team members principles of improvement and then help them to apply those principles.

Done for You—This is as it suggests. You do the work for the client because they don't want to or they can't.

Here's a bit more about when you would consider each of the approaches.

ADVISOR

Because the Advisor role is rather light-touch for the consultant, the client will need to take on the burden of actually doing the work. The consultant in the Advisor role could meet with the CEO in a one-on-one session for a day in person once per quarter, with regular phone calls in between. The consultant could have a client project team that he/she is advising, and they can have in-person meetings or calls.

The consultant and client get into dialogue about ideas, problems, challenges, etc., and the consultant shares perspectives and concepts, might help solve problems, determines specific strategies to implement, and then gives specific action steps for the client to take on. In the Advisor role, the consultant could utilize some coaching skills to help guide the client to discovering their own answer, but they really need to make sure they are being somewhat directive with their advice.

This approach is appropriate when there is not a lot of consultant time allocated to the client. For example, if they budget two days a month for six months of on-site support, it's difficult for the consultant to do anything other than play an Advisor role during that time. The goals of the consulting engagement might be more tied to who the consultant could spend time with from the client team, rather than specific changes in operating or financial metrics. With that said, the consultant might define some actions that will lead to visible improvement in the operational and financial metrics. They will need to direct the client on what they are to actually do, because they are the ones to do it. The consultant can hold them accountable by establishing a rhythm of check-ins along the way, but ultimately it is up to the client to do the work.

The Advisor role is a reasonable option to consider when you already have a relationship with the client, perhaps after you have completed some other longer-term projects. You know the players and they know you. You have already established rapport and trust. They know you can add value and help them. They just need a little more support from you to keep them on track.

This is a great role to play for an extended period of time. You might build the on-going role into a contract agreement with the client right up front so they know after the main components of a major project are over they will still have access to you or your team to support them, keep them on track, and answer their questions.

One famous example of a consultant playing an Advisor role is Dr. W. Edward Deming, the American statistician who transformed production methodologies during World War II as his statistical quality control methods helped to create high productivity and quality levels in U.S. manufacturing plants. Deming is also credited for teaching these same principles in Japan, which led to many of the principles today known as the Toyota Production System and Six Sigma. Pete studied under Dr. Deming during the early 1990s. Dr. Deming's class at at the NYU Stern School of Business was held on Monday afternoons because he lived in Washington, DC and commuted each Monday morning, then had clients he advised Tuesday through Friday.

DONE WITH YOU

The Done with You model is one where you are side by side with the client resources. It works well with a longer-term project that has a lot of deliverables for operational and financial improvement. Anything that requires internal process change and employee buy-in to changes is a signal that the Done with You model is appropriate. Change management is more complicated than many people realize and requires extra training of people in the new processes, extra facilitation to gain buy-in and support, and extra follow-up to make sure the process changes are working.

When there's a huge component of new principles to inject into the company, Done with You is the way to go because you will need to conduct formal training sessions in addition to the informal coaching and guidance that you provide.

The ideal infrastructure for Done with You engagements includes a clear set of roles within the client resources. You will want to have client executive sponsors identified who will support the client's teams and be the point person to interact with the consultants on managing the implementation strategy. You would identify a number of different project teams to drive the different elements of the strategy and have ownership for results. You will have team leaders, perhaps internal facilitators, and team members—all identified and an extension of your consulting project.

DONE FOR YOU

Done for You is the appropriate model when the client wants the results, but doesn't have the time or know-how to deliver the results. You might have deep expertise and the client wants you to come in, conduct the analyses, and share your recommendations. Then you leave them the to-do list as you depart. Other times, you will be asked to deliver results on an on-going basis because the client trusts that you can do a great job and deliver value—and they don't have anyone currently available on their staff who can do the role.

When Pete was at McKinsey, he was part of a number of engagements where the consulting team was to conduct a set of observations and analyze the client's current processes as an input to a larger strategy development exercise. The client was needed to provide information and answer questions, but they really didn't have the expertise to do the work that the consultants would do. That was a know-how gap, and sometimes a capacity gap.

Terri has a lot of clients where she simply handles their Facebook marketing. She has some proprietary approaches that are very effective. If the client wants the results, Terri's team delivers.

VIRTUAL VERSUS TRADITIONAL CONSULTING

If you are only familiar with consultants who are on site with their clients training, teaching, facilitating, and supporting, you can expand your awareness to realize that there are consultants who never leave their home offices. Similarly, if you are a consultant who spends all day on the phone in jeans and bunny slippers remotely talking to and supporting your clients, you might be surprised to learn that some consultants venture out into the wild to visit their clients in person.

The traditional model was to be an on-site consultant who visited and supported the client in person. The reality is that clients want a lot of hands on support, and working with clients in person may be the dominant consulting approach for you. In today's world with greater access to technology, however, more consultants are building their businesses where they can have clients without traveling. And even if you prefer the traditional consulting model, there may be opportunities for you to incorporate more remote client arrangements. You have to decide what type of consultant you want to be—it could be one or the other, or both. Life isn't always an either/or choice—it could be *both/and.*

For the road warrior consultants who follow the traditional model of traveling to clients (and this could be you for a while), recognize the pros and cons of heavy travel. You're away from home a lot. You live in hotels and sleep on airplanes. Your client could have multiple locations. If you're located on the East Coast and the client who asks for your help happens to be located on the West Coast, and they want you there in person for a meeting the next day, guess what? That means you are hopping on an airplane, renting a car, staying in a hotel, and sacrificing a lot of sleep in order to serve their needs.

Pete has had red eye flights to Brazil or Europe where he then had to exit the airport and go straight to the client site for a twelve- to sixteen-hour day, then had to be on a plane the following morning to head somewhere else. This isn't bragging; it's a warning. This might happen in your consulting career, too. The upside of this is that you make a lot of money and collect a lot of air miles and hotel points. The downside is that this type of travel could wreck havoc on one's personal health and well-being—and possibly relationships.

When you show up on site, you might be working with senior executives, or you might be working with managers, supervisors, and work teams that actually do the work on the process you are there to improve. That means you could show up in a suit and tie, or you might be working in an environment where you're dressed in business casual or jeans with your sleeves rolled up, flip charts and markers in hand, with Post-it notes, and work teams going through and solving problems actively.

You might find that you're there to facilitate one- or two-day meetings, you might be there for a one to two-week diagnostic, or you might be there for a number of weeks back to back to support some implementation of various strategies that you present to them. In fact, for larger consultant projects you might have multiple people on a team, not just you. As your business grows, it might be that it's not even you delivering the work after the initial contract is defined, but your team is on-site delivering the work.

Terri does a lot of her work these days virtually. She and her team, use webinars, teleconferences, and videoconferences so they don't need to travel.

Pete mostly relies on his team of resources to be on site conducting the necessary work, but will be available for some diagnostics and important progress review discussions.

It is possible for you to provide your consulting services remotely, and not leave your home office. With today's technology, it is easy to think of phone, Skype, or other video conference meetings where you can communicate, share your content, discuss issues, and help solve problems without being on site or in person. Because consulting is largely about solving problems, if you can find a way to be effective at solving your client's problems and providing them a huge sigh of relief while working remotely, then you will have a long and successful career with a nice work/life balance.

Go out of your way to discuss and introduce the concept of holding meetings virtually from the very beginning, and work this into your consulting approach. That will help your lifestyle, limit some of your travel, and likely be more flexible for your clients.

Think of this, if you have a large corporate client with multiple locations, they may also be flying their people into one location to be part of the meetings you are facilitating. It would save them tons of travel costs, as it does you, if your workshop or problem-solving session can be done remotely. The sooner that you build that into your model and get the client comfortable with interacting with you in this manner, the easier it will be to go and work with them effectively over time.

As you are interviewing prospective clients, be sure to ask where the employees are located and if are all coming into an office. This is easier done right from the beginning of your interactions, rather than when contract negotiations are in place. Then you can work remote support into your agreements up front. Workplace trends are changing, and you will need to adapt just as your clients are. In particular, many Millennials prefer a flexible work arrangement and their employers are allowing it.

While consulting is a service business, you might consider adding products to your consulting services, such as live training programs or audios and videos. If you do have products, then you'll want to talk to your attorney about copyrights so that your products can be protected. Subsequently, when you're developing products for one of your clients using your own intellectual property, you want to make sure your work is protected and who owns rights to the material. We speak more on this in Chapter 8.

**Remember, for bonus resources
related to this chapter, go to:**

www.TheUltimateGamePlanBook.com/resources

SECTION III

• • • • • • •

HOW TO POWER UP YOUR CONSULTING BUSINESS

This section is super important. The Power Up Formula is the foundation of building your business and enabling you to skyrocket your revenues and profits. We used the Power Up Formula to construct the agenda for our live workshop, *Power Up Your Consulting Business,* and have taught it in webinars.

As you review the Power Up Formula, think about where you are in your business right now. Take notes on your ideas about how you will use this formula for immediate client benefit as you grow your business.

CHAPTER 6

* * * * * * *

THE POWER UP FORMULA

When we named our inaugural workshop, *Power Up Your Consulting Business*, we had already created the Power Up Formula. This formula is the key to your long-term growth and business success as you create an outstanding reputation for delivering amazing value to clients.

That's really vital in everything you do in your consulting business. You always want to have your clients feel like you have gone above and beyond for them. And, let your results speak for themselves—as long as you deliver the goods, your clients will love you and tell everyone about you.

Here is the Power Up Formula in its most simple form.

Get Clients + Deliver High Impact = Higher Fees + More Clients

This formula repeats. Each time you get more clients, you can then deliver high impact and continue to see your fees and number of clients increase, which means your revenue will sky-rocket!

Let us break this down for you so that you can see how this all fits together and is relevant to your business today—no matter where you are in your company's maturity from brand new consultant to seasoned veteran.

GET CLIENTS

Getting clients seems obvious, but when you're a brand new consultant breaking into this field or an old pro who is launching a new service, it might not be so easy to land a client. If you're a new consultant, you clearly need to bring in some clients right away. Real work is in order immediately. It's not about finding office space, getting your website right, or designing business cards. It's about getting into action with a real client.

So where could you go out and get a client? Perhaps a friend would be willing to let you do a project for them. It could be that you offer your services at a fee level way below what you want to charge even though you know you're worth a lot more. It could be you get lucky and land a client at your normal current fee. No matter what, you have to go out and get a client project because you are not an academic theorist—you are a business consultant who solves real problems and creates huge financial benefit for your clients. And while you deserve to be paid well for your work, you still have to prove it with real client projects!

If you have been at this a while, this step in the formula still holds true. You need that "next" client, which is why we will teach you to always be marketing. Use the marketing tools we will describe in the chapters within the next section to attract clients to you.

If you are branching out to deliver a new service offering, you need to get your first or next client in that area just as you would a brand new consultant. So, let's say you've been doing strategy consulting for the last five years and have a stable reputation in this area, but you have not ever really provided consulting support for implementation. Then you hire some consulting resources who are excellent at execution—do you think it will be easy to simply have a list of clients ready to pay full fees for execution projects if you are not yet known for this type of work? If you think it will be easy, think again. It's important for this new capability to build your reputation and a case history of examples to give your future clients the confidence that you know what you're talking about. Go get a client in that area that is new to you.

DELIVER HIGH IMPACT

Now that you have a client project, it's up to you to deliver the goods. You have to do whatever it takes to blow away your client's expectations. You want them to giggle with joy at the value you delivered to them. Then while they are so happy, ask them for a video testimonial and some referrals.

Delivering high impact is about value. Value to your client is going to be where the benefit they receive is in excess of what they invested. If you have a history of delivering more value to clients than they invest in having you help them, then you are on the right track. It's far better to deliver multiples of value, such as twice, five times, or even ten times their investment.

When you are working with a brand new client, you want to really knock their socks off. First impressions mean everything in the consulting world, especially because it is such a relationship business. Think of how you can go above and beyond in every possible interaction.

For example, if your new client wants to call you in the evening to talk through issues, then that might be the highest leverage activity for you to conduct to give them the perception of amazing value. If after you've developed the relationship, your client is still calling during off-hours and it has become excessive then you can collectively discuss boundaries and how to work together. However, early in your relationship, do your best to be available if that will help your client recognize you deliver amazing value.

Delivering multiples of what your new client invested is easier to do when it is a friend that has agreed to launch a project with you at a super discount compared to the fee level you normally set for client work. If the project is normally $30,000, but you billed them just $15,000 as a win-win arrangement (where they get the consulting support and you get a client example), then when you deliver them $60,000 of value it's a 4x Return on Investment (ROI) rather than just a 2x ROI. Both ROI numbers are outstanding. It's just that the order of magnitude is more impressive, so be prepared to share the ROI multiple as well as the absolute dollar value in any case studies or marketing materials where you describe your impact.

Remember to get a testimonial as some "social proof" about your successful project. If your client is willing to be video recorded, this is the most powerful way to have future clients relate to the work you've delivered. Imagine your client looking at the camera with a huge smile on his/her face, speaking authentically and from the heart about your impact. They could also write a letter that talks about the results you delivered for them—again, authentically and from the heart.

Furthermore, the best source of referrals is a satisfied client who is thrilled about the work you did for them. They may independently think of you at a cocktail party or networking event when someone asks if you know of a consulting resource who can help solve their problem; however, the reality is people are just darn busy these days. Prompt them with the request, "Do you know anyone who might have a similar business challenge that you think we could help? Would you be willing to introduce me?"

When someone is willing to make an introduction on your behalf, do what you can to simplify their efforts by providing them a pre-written biography, your contact information, and any other information that you want to have as part of your how you're introduced. A simple way to do this is with a short thank you email to your client, like this: "Thanks for agreeing to introduce me to Mr/Ms. X at the ABC Company. Here's something you can copy and paste to make it easy for you. Feel free to edit this for your own words."

HIGHER FEES

As you build your reputation for delivering tremendous value, you will see more potential clients interested in your service. The simple economics of supply and demand suggest that as demand goes up with a fixed supply, the price will go up. Assume this will happen for you, too. Here's why:

If you're at full capacity and people are still calling and asking for your help, then clearly it's time to declare a higher fee. If it's too high, then some people will decline your service, but if you're at full capacity then you are totally fine with it. To illustrate, if you double your fee and less than half of your potential projects disappear, then you will bring in more revenue for your business. (2x the fee with half the projects is the same amount of revenue.)

The reality about setting consulting fees is that the fee is largely psychological, both for you and your client. You will set fees as a function of what you are worth. If you have a belief that the work you provide is worth just $1,000 per day, shaped because you're only familiar with consultants who charge $1,000 per day for their services, then you will probably be super uncomfortable asking for $4,000 per day no matter how good you are. You have to break through your hidden beliefs about what you could be charging so that you are not artificially holding yourself back.

You also need to make sure that your clients appreciate your value. If you want $20,000 for a five-day project, they will do the math and come up with a rate of $4,000 per day. Until they are clear about the value the project will deliver, they could play around with figures and might then decide that is too much money for them to spend on your consulting services. Some business leaders will take their salary and divide by the number of working days per year and conclude, "Wait a minute! I don't make that much per day so why would I pay that to someone else..." While it seems obvious that this is an upside down way to think of it, many business leaders get stuck thinking of consulting service as an expense rather than as an investment. It's your job to make sure they are thinking of it the right way.

The burden of demonstrating your value is on your shoulders. This is why it's so critical to have client examples to use in your conversations with your prospects. This is also why you would ideally have a chance to study your client's processes so that you can predict the impact to their financials (maybe in a paid diagnostic!). If you are able to show how that $20,000 investment will deliver between $40,000 and $60,000 of benefit this year, then it won't matter at all what the rate is—they will say yes.

We have demonstrated again and again, in our own businesses and those of our clients, that the Power Up Formula is the best way to continue to grow your business and increase your fees over time as long as you deliver the highest possible impact that you possibly can—always. This is a value proposition where clients are paying your fees, and yet no matter how high your fees are you deliver value that is a huge multiple of the fees they pay you. The result is that your clients are experiencing an enormous ROI and are always happy with your work.

Because of the high ROI that you deliver to them, they continue to see you as a partner for them whenever they have challenges or problems that they need to solve. They also seek your advice when you build solid relationships based on value because they trust you. They trust your opinion, they trust your point of view, they trust that you are able to deliver on these ideas that you have.

Frequently, a client does not have perspectives outside of their own immediate company, immediate network, or immediate past experiences. That is one of the ways that a consultant can add enormous value because a consultant has multiple clients that they serve and, therefore, has the chance to experience multiple problems in different business settings and different industries with different sets of people and companies. All of this experience translates into you and your firm becoming a versatile expert that can bring new thought processes, ideas, principles, and perspectives into your client situation. When you are able to teach them your principles and ideas, guide them to solve their most challenging problems, and help them to grow their top line and bottom line financials, they will fall in love with you forever. Beyond falling in love with you, they also will share their story of working with you with other people. This is where your referral network begins to grow.

Clearly, the important thing with your consulting business is not just to feel satisfied that you've scored a gig and are collecting some revenues from the invoice that you just cut. You really must have a bigger perspective than just your immediate paycheck. You are no longer an employee working for someone else. This is your firm and your reputation on the line. So with this in mind, no matter what fee level you are at today, it's critical for you to always deliver the highest possible impact for your client so that they can experience the value that you deliver to them.

MORE CLIENTS

The other element of delivering great work and building a solid reputation is that you will enjoy that steady stream of potential clients coming your way. We will teach you in the next section about developing and using different marketing strategies that leverage your solid reputation. You will become known as the expert in your area, and companies with the business challenges that you solve will seek you out.

With your stellar performance for your clients, you will create an inventory of success stories, testimonials, case studies, and referrals. You will find ways to use these both directly and indirectly to enjoy the extra client projects as you continue to build your business.

THE POWER UP FORMULA CONTINUES TO TURN

The best part is that as you continue to get new clients, you will always strive to deliver high impact and exceed clients' expectations as you deliver amazing value. This will lead you to further grow your reputation and inventory of success stories, which brings you more clients even as you continue to raise your fees.

In the next two sections, we talk about everything you need to do so that you can get more clients (Section IV) and then deliver high impact and awesome value (Section V). Now that we've whet your whistle, jump into the details in the next section and learn how easy it can be for you to always be marketing and create a steady stream of clients coming your way—and Power Up your business.

Remember, for bonus resources
related to this chapter, go to:

www.TheUltimateGamePlanBook.com/resources

SECTION IV

• • • • • • •

GET CLIENTS WITH THE PACK MODEL

As we've been saying all along, systems create success—and save time and money. The PACK Model is the best way to build your business and get to work.

P is for *Position*—What unique position could you hold in the market?

A is for *Attract*—Rather than push yourself on potential clients, think of drawing clients to you as a moth to a flame, or a bee to a flower.

C is for *Convert*—Now that you've garnered your prospect's attention, what will it take for them to commit?

K is for *Keep*—It's more lucrative to develop long-term relationships to keep your clients than to court new clients on a continual basis.

By implementing the PACK model, your process of getting and keeping clients will be streamlined. We'll show you how in the next few chapters.

CHAPTER 7

· · · · · · ·

KNOW YOUR POSITION—CREATING YOUR BRAND

To truly power up your consulting business, you must now start thinking about your brand. Your brand is your public face—it's your position in the market place. Brand is the identity you select to set yourself apart from all of the other consultants so that clients will decide to choose you. Brands cannot just say that they are better or the brand of choice because no one believes self-promotion. The best way to create a brand that will help you get clients and build your business is to first determine specifically and exactly who your target audience is. Then it's important to define what your consulting does that is better than anyone else in the industry or unique and different from all other consultants.

If you spend the time determining your specific niche and how you are unique, then you can completely dominate your market. Instead of promoting yourself and constantly hunting for new clients, by determining your exact target audience and your point of differentiation, you will make it easy for new clients to find you.

CORE UNIQUE POSITIONING STATEMENT

We teach the clients in our mastermind how to create a Core Unique Positioning Statement (CUPS). This statement creates the branding for our clients and sets them apart from everybody else that is doing consulting. There is always something that you do differently and that you do better than other consultants. This can be a skill set or a trait that you have. Begin thinking about the practical value that you bring to your consulting clients. We are not only talking about what you do practically to get clients results, but also the perceived of what you do bigger, better, and greater. Creating a Core Unique Positioning Statement that incorporates your extrinsic and intrinsic value works like a magnet and helps to pull potential prospects towards you. We label this technique reverse marketing. Reverse marketing is where you have prospects coming to you and raising their hands to say they are interested in your consulting services instead of you chasing after them. A Core Unique Positioning Statement becomes your client attraction magnet.

Positioning will distinguish your consulting business from all of the competition and set you up to be the preferred choice in your area of expertise with your niche market segment. When we help our mastermind clients to create their Core Unique Positioning Statements, we make sure the statement has distinct value for their target market and serves the biggest issues on their potential client's minds. By assisting our clients in crafting the perfect statement, we state their clearly meaningful differences and define their value to their ideal target audience so they become the consultant of choice in their industry.

We go further in their marketing and branding to support, with real evidence, how the consultant produces the results stated in their Core Unique Positioning. Once our clients have this sentence, they are literally in control of market perception and are establishing authority in their consulting niche. The right statement tells employees, investors, prospects, clients, business partners, the media, and competitors very clearly what your company does and helps make it much easier for clients to purchase your consulting services. The statement is the foundation of reverse marketing so take this very seriously. Do not say anything in your statement that you cannot easily demonstrate. Be certain the statement is based on absolute truth. When crafting this statement, be focused on potential prospects and clients, ensure that it is process-based, and confirm it does not contain jargon. Also make sure it is original and not filled with hype.

Here's an example of a poorly written CUPS:

We help businesses improve their bottom line with our best practices consulting program.

Revised and much improved:

We are the only dental consulting firm that uses the proprietary Azuma Method to increase patient visits and your bottom line - guaranteed.

Innovative positioning that communicates a customer centric statement and that differentiates your consulting with real benefits that your prospects are seeking—and that shows how you are their solution—will have clients coming and asking for your services. To create your statement, think about emerging issues that your target audience is facing or will shortly face. You want to capitalize on trends in the market place. What threats might your prospects be up against now or in the very near future? How can the core competencies of your business consulting help prospects? Keep these answers in mind when you craft your Core Unique Positioning Statement.

In order to market effectively, you must know the exact problems you solve and for which target audience you solve those problems. You also must understand your niche market and how they purchase consulting services. We have our mastermind clients learn how their prospects buy, discover who their prospects listen to, and find out the benefits clients are seeking. Then with their unique differences and attributes, our clients use their positioning strategy to gain their target audiences attention.

It's best not to outsource this exercise to someone else to write this statement for you. If you do need assistance, it is best to hire someone who has massive experience to help you craft your statement as this is the very key to all of your marketing success. And remember, this is a dynamic statement. As your business grows and transforms, so will your CUPS.

CREATING YOUR CORE UNIQUE POSITIONING STATEMENT

* What is your expertise?
* What are you an expert in?
* What do you take for granted and do automatically?
* What comes easily, naturally to you?
* How is your life experience equivalent to expertise?
* What is your expertise and how can you use that in a business environment?

Additionally, to clarify your expertise, look at your life decade by decade and ask, "What did I enjoy during those decades?" Notice the themes and the thread that ties the decades together. Also, have someone you know look at your notes, and ask what connection they see.

And then the question that seems to be the dead giveaway— What is the market asking of you? Our editor began coaching people in writing and became a publishing consultant after the question: "What do you do?" And when she answered, "I'm a writer." The usual response was, "I've always wanted to write." She's been coaching aspiring writers for nearly two decades because of noting what the market wanted from her.

INTEGRATING YOUR CORE UNIQUE POSITIONING STATEMENT

Once you have this statement you need to integrate it into all of your marketing. Present your brand to the world, by sharing your identity and integrating the core unique position your company holds on your website, your letterhead, your business cards, in PowerPoint templates you use during presentations, in brochures and flyers, or other leave behind materials or handouts.

Your brand is based on this statement, and this becomes your public view. Before you develop any materials, take time to craft your Core Unique Positioning Statement and then use the statement in all of your marketing so that you have the same brand identity to communicate your message to the public. Everything you present must be aligned with this statement right down to your email signature file and voice mail message. Let the public know, through your Core Unique Positioning Statement, who your company is and how you help them, and how you do that differently from any other consultant. This will help the market find you, both on and off line. Your statement must be so clear that prospects can tell immediately if they want to work with you as a respected authority in their field. Through your positioning and branding, prospects will have a way to think about you, to recognize how you can help them, why you help them, and then take some inspired action to demonstrate their interest to work with you.

A great Core Unique Positioning Statement will increase the number of people who will raise their hands to work with you and identify your prospects to you. Since prospects will come to you already interested in what you provide, you will be able to close them quickly. Remember, all of your marketing will depend on creating a perfect Core Unique Positioning Statement. Our mastermind clients have increased their demand—and therefore their profitability—by having their perfect Core Unique Positioning Statements.

YOUR ONLINE PRESENCE

Certainly, you must have an online presence to be in business today and to be taken seriously so once you have the perfect statement think about your business's web domain. Your domain name is just as important as the content on your website and needs to be thought out very carefully as part of your overall marketing and branding strategy. You will be using your website domain on your business cards, in your email signatures, in your letterhead, at the footer of your proposal documents, etc. When prospects visit your website, you must be certain your site reflects your Core Unique Positioning, your identity, and what is special about you. Prospects need to know who you are and how you work with them, as well as the big benefit they will get as result of hiring you. One of the most important items to include on your website is how prospects contact you. You want to have a clickable phone number as well as a contact form, your office address, and your email. Make it very easy for contacts to get in touch with you in multiple ways and encourage them to call.

On your website also include some content that prospects can easily consume and digest so they can see that you are a credible expert without you saying so. Having your prospects draw the conclusion is much more valuable than you telling them you are a credible expert. We suggest your website has blogs as articles and also contains videos as well. The goal of your website is to back up your Core Unique Positioning Statement by letting prospects consume some of your expertise and to get to know you a bit better. Over time, they will continue to get to know you, and it is likely they will then hire you.

Remember, for bonus resources related to this chapter, go to:

www.TheUltimateGamePlanBook.com/resources

CHAPTER 8

• • • • • • •

ATTRACTING CLIENTS BY DEMONSTRATING EXPERTISE

AS A CONSULTANT YOU WANT TO demonstrate that you are an expert in your field of consulting, and you want to do that without being braggadocios—and without talking about the great "guru" that you are and how fabulous you are. One of the best ways that you can demonstrate your expertise—and build lead generation—is by creating content that you can give to prospects, either in print form or via the internet for distribution. But first let's spend some time on the concept of lead generation—and why it's important—because for most consultants there is a high level of anxiety around "getting clients."

LEAD GENERATION

Here's the secret: You can create a high-income consulting business where you don't even need a lot of clients. It is possible you could land a corporate client for $100,000, $200,000, $300,000, $400,000, or $500,000—or sign a client worth multiple millions of dollars over the life of your relationship with them.

It is also possible you may land some smaller clients depending on your business model. Smaller clients may bring you

$10,000 a month or $4,000 a month, or sometimes even under that. Remember, even a $10,000 a month client reaps $120,000 per year. And, multiple smaller clients who don't require a lot of your time also add up to a lot of revenue. The key is to know *who* your prospects are and *where* to find them.

Instead of trying to get thousands of people to respond to your marketing, it is more important that you market to the exact kind of people who are very interested in your services and then get them, through reverse marketing, to raise their hands because they want to work with you and your company. We believe in setting up your marketing so that you do not have to do a lot of follow-up. Rather than trying to bring in massive numbers of prospects, the goal is to bring in the right prospects who are very interested in potentially hiring you and your company—and then doing a great job with the clients that do hire you so that they stay long term.

If you identify the right segment of the market and you really know their biggest problem—and you have a solution for that problem—then you can spend your marketing time, energy, and focus speaking and/or writing only to the right market that is most probable to raise their hands and who will hire you more quickly. This is why we recommend focusing all of your marketing on your specific market segment—who is most likely to hire you—*and who is likely to pay the most*. We believe you set yourself up for success when you are working on closing deals that are easier to land versus those that will be slower and harder to close because they require convincing. The game of marketing is having a lot of very interested prospects, knowing some will close now and others will need nurturing to close in the future. The model we teach will help you with the people making the decision to hire you. Always remember the most essential element of your marketing—both online and offline—is that prospects believe they will get the results, which are the answers to their biggest problems, by using your consulting services. And to ensure them that you are the right consultant for their job, you must establish a high level of expertise, and you can do that through a variety of platforms.

THE CONSUMER AWARENESS GUIDE

We recommend to all the clients in our mastermind that they create what we call a "Consumer Awareness Guide." This guide can be written or it can be a video or audio. It can even be all three. The purpose of the guide is to make people aware of the things to look for when hiring the specific type consulting services that you provide. For example, if you are an IT consultant your Consumer Awareness Guide would include the things to look for before you hire an IT consultant. You might even title it something like "The 5 Deadly Mistakes People Make when Hiring an IT Consultant." The guide would then show your expertise and highlight the deadly mistakes. It serves as a public service of your company. Guides are made available as free downloads and also can be handed out. You can use the content in the guides to make DVDs, CDs, or Mp3s to give away. The concept is that you create a Consumer Awareness Guide to demonstrate that you are aware of the problems and mistakes in the industry—and that you also know how to solve them.

To see an example, you can download our Consumer Awareness Guide titled *"How To Know if Consulting Is Right for You and If It Is, What To Do To Get Started Quickly"* at www.businessconsultantinstitute.com.

MAGAZINE ARTICLES

Writing magazine articles also demonstrates expertise. Advertisements, on the other hand, never make you appear credible, as people do not believe what ads have to say. Ads act as promotional information where people talk about how wonderful they are, and what a great expert they are in their fields. People read these as clear self-promotion, and self-promotion just does not work nowadays. Articles, however, give you enhanced credibility. When people read an article, they believe what is written in the article, then they look at who wrote the article and how to make contact with the author. Be sure to include contact info, such as the name of your company and your website. Writing articles for trade publications and magazines online or offline is a very important strategy. *Writer's Market* is an excellent source for finding all those in publication. The natural fit, however, would be to write for those magazines that you read. And if you're already crunched on time, you can hire a ghostwriter to create content for you. It may, however, take a few articles with you doing some heavier editing for that writer to be able to mimic your writer's voice. Eventually, though, this could be win-win. You gain visibility and credibility without having to invest a lot of time into content creation.

BLOGS AND WEBSITE ARTICLES

Much like magazine articles, blogs give you expert status. Even if you just write a blog once a week, even short ones, you can enhance your visibility. Blogging has brought us a high number of leads and enhanced our credibility. We recommend that you blog regularly and use the keywords and the topics that your target audience is using in their searches. For example, our posts often include keywords such as business leaders, continuous improvement, goals, leadership, and productivity. Guest blogging on other people's blogs and also blogging on LinkedIn or Huffington Post can enhance your credibility as well. This in turn will boost your website and social media presence.

In addition to blogging, you can write longer articles and place these on your website and submit them to other websites. When you write articles for other people's blogs, or make valuable comments on industry forums by responding to other people's conversations, your visibility increases and you gain credible expert status. You may even decide to approach your local newspaper about writing a column. Reach out to the editor with an introductory letter containing the topic for a possible article and explain why you're the person to write it. This might just lead to a steady gig with weekly visibility. Again, *Writer's Market* offers tips on how this is best done. Often editors like to have an extra copy on hand in case there is a hole in the content on publication day. Even if a column doesn't materialize immediately, you may solve a problem for an editor by offering your blog posts as a ready-made article submission. Just remember, offer value and omit the glaring self-promotion.

BOOKS

Writing a book is a great way to get your ideal target audience to know more about you and your services. We strongly recommend a print book as e-books have become over-used. We tell our mastermind clients to give away their books because books enhance their credible expert status. Books are often referred to as the golden business card, and your target audience likely will raise their hands and contact you after they've gotten to know you through your written word. As a bonus, once you create a book, it is much easier to get booked on television and for speaking gigs. The reason Terri has been a guest expert on television over and over again is that she uses her books to make the television stations aware of her credible expert status.

PRESS RELEASES

One thing you want to do regularly is to send out press releases. Pay attention to the hot topics in newspapers and magazines, and then come up with something to say that is of interest about those topics. One example is an expert in bullying in the workplace who was launching into leadership consulting. After the Columbine disaster they contacted the press. They landed prime space in national magazines and newspapers. This client was a brand-new consultant and they kick-started their entire consulting business that way.

RADIO

We always tell our clients to get on the radio because getting radio interviews booked is actually very easy. Pitch radio stations both locally as well as nationally about new story ideas. Terri has a radio show that also plays on the iHeart radio network. Her show is called "The Terri Levine Show" and her tagline is "Business Advice You Can Take to the Bank." This tagline attracts her target audience because they know she is discussing topics they want to know about.

TELEVISION

Television is not that hard to get on either. You just need to have a well-crafted pitch, and know how to present that pitch to TV in the right way. So don't be afraid to approach television stations as well. Reach out to the producer of the show where you're interested in appearing. Again, focus on making their job easier because you have information that will appeal to their audience. Always add value. When you do that, you could become a regular—or even the "go-to" person on your area of expertise.

VIDEOS

Another great strategy is creating many (we recommend 100) one-minute videos. These videos share your knowledge on the topics you know about. After you've completed each one (not the entire hundred or so) then upload them to your own You-Tube channel. These one-minute videos give expert information and at the end you say who the video is brought to you by, giving your name and your website. Post these to other platforms as well, such as your business Facebook page, LinkedIn, industry-related group forums, and more.

One of the things Terri did in her business was to create over 100 one-minute videos on top topics of interest to her audience. Some examples are: "How to Hire a Virtual Assistant" or "Should You be An LLC or an S Corp?" Terri then uploaded them to her YouTube channel. She also shared them on social media to reach her target audience. Many of the clients in our mastermind use this technique to create leads on a regular basis.

PODCASTS

Audios can be a very important strategy because they become viral on the Internet when shared. In addition to getting your voice heard by the masses as a podcast guest, you might even consider having your own podcast where you demonstrate the knowledge that you have. Be sure to interview credible experts in the field that have big names. Once you attach your name to a credible expert, you instantly raise your authority. Several years back, Terri wrote a book with Steven Covey and Ken Blanchard, who are two top leadership people in the field of consulting. This instantly raised her credibility as a consultant and the amount of money she was able to charge for consulting engagements also increased. This is why you want to bring guests to your podcast to interview them.

WEBINARS AND TELESEMINARS

Another tactic to use are webinars. We host many webinars to share our knowledge and experience, and we do not make a sales pitch at the end. We simply give people a lot of value so they can decide if they want to raise their hands for our services. If you are not comfortable with webinars, you can use teleseminars on a phone conference line. You might even want to try Zoom or YouTube Live if you would like to do video conferencing. Amping up this idea, consider creating a summit where you bring your leads together with other business owners for expert trainings.

SPEAKING

You can attract an influx of serious leads through speaking engagements around your target topics. Speaking can include anything from doing lunch and learn presentations for businesses, to giving seminars on your own, or speaking at other people's seminars or conferences as a keynote speaker or breakout sessions.

Offering to speak at the Rotary, Chambers of Commerce, and other organizations will raise your expert profile. Lunch and learns will provide companies the opportunity to see you in action and plant the seed of possibility for them to contact you when the need arises. Workshops, events, and masterminds are also avenues for reaching your target audience. Invite key decision makers in the organizations you want to work with. Once prospects are a part of what you are doing, they will be engaged and impressed by your expertise. Just be certain to avoid going into sales mode. This point is critically important: Remember, the way that you demonstrate yourself as an expert is not by talking about how great you are, it is by showing people how great you are.

NETWORKING

It's wise to be very active at networking, either at local weekly meetings or by attending conferences aimed at your target market. Consider having a booth at conferences as well. We also recommend that you attend association meetings where your target audience can be found. You might consider becoming an active member of the Chamber of Commerce if your target audience belongs to your local chamber. We always tell our clients not to be *just* members. Instead, we urge them to be active members of anything they join.

BUILD A SOCIAL MEDIA PLATFORM

FACEBOOK

The best way to get the right prospects is on Facebook via Facebook business page posts, pay-per-click, being the leader of your own niched Facebook group, and Facebook Live. These all possibly play a role in your social media plan. Facebook is the best place, in our experience, to advertise. Facebook is the largest data provider to get the most advanced targeting and is even better than Google "pay-per-click." The opportunity you have with Facebook advertising is that it allows you to find people that need your services and in the demographic you choose. You select the exact kind of audience affluence as well as people, job role, purchase history, and any other essential data. On Facebook, you can even get down to the type of vehicle someone drives.

If you want to reach a certain kind a professional—for example, if you consult to medical professionals—Facebook can identify them. In fact, Facebook has 500 different categories, and it is really not that expensive to advertise directly to your exact niche. We have found Facebook to be one of the best places for advertising. Facebook also allows you to create a custom audience. With a custom audience, you can actually find the exact demographic list to market to. In Terri's consulting business, she was doing a lot of work with dentists and Facebook helped her to get her message directly in front of these professionals. She had lists of dentists with their phone numbers, without the dentists' Facebook profiles. Facebook allowed her to put those phone numbers into Facebook as an upload, and Facebook matched the phone numbers against its entire database and everybody that is on Facebook. It then created a custom audience for her and displayed her pay-per-click ad right in front of her precise target audience.

Sometimes, we use Facebook leads to capture the names and emails of our interested parties and other times we just display a sponsored ad in front of our ideal target audience. We frequently tell Facebook to put our ad in front of the biggest business consultants in our area of expertise audience. Since these people already have the target audience we are trying to reach, all we need to do is identify the main players in our niche, and—boom—we can have our ad run to their followers and friends.

With Facebook, you have an incredible opportunity to get in front of your target audience as long as you have done a good job of identifying them.

LINKEDIN

We also recommend LinkedIn posts, LinkedIn blog posts, setting up your own highly niched LinkedIn group, and pay-per-click advertising on LinkedIn because professionals are easy to find there. LinkedIn also works extremely well because you can get in front of customers the same way on LinkedIn as you can on Facebook. We use our Consumer Awareness Guide in conjunction with the social media ad strategy. Our ads offer the Consumer Awareness Guide as a giveaway.

You might create an ad that says something like: "The Seven Deadly Questions You Didn't Ask Before You Hired a Business Consultant" or "What are the Seven Deadly Questions that You Must Ask a Business Consultant Before You Hire Them?" Using a report like that, and getting the report in front of your target market, allows your audience to then raise their hands if they are interested and compelled to learn more. The Consumer

Awareness Guide makes a great giveaway. You can use any other type of special report or even a template or checklist as your giveaway. Simply post to tell people on LinkedIn about it so they know that your Consumer Awareness Guide is available.

CREATING YOUR UNIQUE FRAMEWORK

Now that you have an idea about the types of mechanisms and platforms for you to share your expertise, we want you to think about your unique and distinctive approach—or framework—to illustrate your expertise in a way that is not like everyone else's.

The problem that many consultants have is that they look just like the next person. From a client perspective, it is confusing for them to know why they would choose one consultant over another if they all look and sound alike. When this occurs, clients make their decisions based solely on price, as opposed to the value that you can deliver to them. You not only want to demonstrate that you are not just an incredible expert, you also want to show that you have a unique point to your consulting by having your own framework, model, or system to differentiate yourself and what you do from what the rest of the consulting world does. When you create your own unique and specialized framework, you can then incorporate that into all of the other mechanisms that we just mentioned like blogs, books, webinars, videos, etc. What's fun about creating a unique framework is that it forces you to be really crisp in your thinking to pull together the steps and processes of your consulting techniques in a way that is comprehensive, cohesive, and easy to deliver. It also is a way for your clients to recognize that your process is different enough to be the one that they want to use and follow. You can read more about frameworks in Chapter 13.

COPYRIGHTS AND TRADEMARKS

Once you establish yourself as an expert and you have created some unique frameworks, models, and systems, you then must be certain you protect that which is uniquely yours with copyrights and trademarks. A copyright is basically protecting your unique work that you have written out in some way. This could be your articles, blogs, books, videos, or audio programs. We go as far as putting a copyright symbol with the date on all of our communications including PowerPoints, and Word documents. We also include the words, "All Rights Reserved" or "All Rights Reserved Worldwide." Have a conversation with your attorney to make sure you are properly protecting all of your work. The ideas here are representative and can get you started so that you know what types of questions to be asking your attorney. Here's our quick disclaimer: Do not take this paragraph or anything in this book as legal advice. It is meant to be the catalyst for you to seek the right type of legal advice.

Trademarks go beyond what copyrights do and protect elements of your business, like your brand logo, your logo, or maybe a catch phrase that describes your business. Something like Nike's "Just Do It" is a trademark. If you have a catchphrase or logo that you want to protect for your business, then you may want to trademark. Discuss seeking trademark protection with your attorney. Trademarks are federally registered, and they are legally protected. While a federal trademark is not mandatory, it can have advantages. Be certain to talk to an attorney to see whether or not you need to have what you are doing trademarked or not, and if it even can be trademarked. Sometimes words and phrases are trademarked and other times they are not. It is also very important not only to just know what kind of mark you want to register. You also must know the services or goods that you wish to register along with the mark.

Because you do need both of those for the application, you want to make sure that whatever it is that you intend to trademark is not already trademarked by somebody else. A lot of word terms may already be trademarked so it is important that you consult an attorney to make sure that whatever you are thinking of trademarking is not already trademarked. That way you are truly protecting your material, your framework, approach model, or system.

YOUR PROPRIETARY PROCESS

An advanced technique we also want to mention here is to suggest displaying your expertise by creating a proprietary process. In Terri's business, for example, she created a transformational in-house process that involves forming what she calls Transformation Teams in companies. The transformation team is a process that has a very distinct approach and that system is actually trademarked. Corporations that really like the system ask her to white label it to them—meaning for a fee, she allows them to use the system and put their brand name on it and use it in-house. They pay her an upfront fee for this, and she also gets a continual fee for them using the system. This is paid to her each and every month. If you do that with a lot of corporations, you will have an impressive passive income stream.

BUILD YOUR MARKETING MUSCLE

Since you make your money by consulting engagements, clients mean revenues and profits—and are the lifeblood of your business. You must continuously be marketing to prospects as well as nurturing your current and past client relationships. Without clients, you will be out of business, and you cannot even make the claim that you are in business when you do not have clients. However, marketing will bring you a steady stream of clients who are willing to invest in your business consulting services. Clearly, clients are the greatest asset in your business so creating marketing systems that consistently attract potential clients are necessary to watch your business—and your profits grow.

If you are new to business consulting, you need to attract your first clients. To get your first clients, you must create a marketing plan and implementation calendar. Your consulting business, regardless of what stage of business you are at, must utilize effective marketing systems. Marketing is what will bring you leads and leads are what convert into clients and where you will obtain your consulting revenues.

Many business consultants don't understand marketing and use marketing techniques that do not work, or are costly. You must have an effective marketing engine working for you that brings you a stream of consulting prospects. Marketing can include everything from ads, newsletters, websites, sales letters, direct mail, brochures, and flyers. Marketing will also include any staff you dedicate to sales and customer service, signage, letterhead, email signature file, social media posts, business cards, etc. Every representation of your consulting company, and every contact you have with prospects or clients, is marketing. Terri often says to attendees of our live *Power Up Your Consulting Business* events that everything is marketing and marketing is everything.

Marketing will determine the success of your consulting business so you want to be certain that you have the marketing skills to be able to attract clients in a fast, cost-efficient and proven way. Marketing takes your quality service—consulting—and puts that service in front of ideal prospects who have the need for your business consulting services.

When you have the right service, placed in front of the right prospects, along with the right message that solves the problem your target audience has, you will be able to create a very successful consulting business. Marketing begins the minute you identify the problem your target audience needs solved that your consulting service will fill. Then you have to decide on the media that will reach your niche audience so you can get your Core Unique Positioning Statement (refer to Chapter 7) in front of them. Once that occurs, they can get to know your company and services and relate to your clear competitive advantage.

Every one of the techniques we mentioned in this chapter will assist you in getting clients and you don't have to do them all. We suggest you take three techniques—selecting those that you will really enjoy doing—and start with those three. Track what's working and what's not. Then if you need more strategies to replace the ones that don't work, go back through the chapter and select another platform. A lot of marketing is testing!

Remember, for bonus resources
related to this chapter, go to:

www.TheUltimateGamePlanBook.com/resources

CHAPTER 9

• • • • • • •

THE ART OF CONVERTING

ONCE YOU HAVE ATTRACTED YOUR ideal prospects, the next thing that happens, ideally, is that they convert themselves into paying clients. You don't want to sell people and convince or manipulate them into using your products and services.

Instead, you want them to have come to you. This is what you learned from the attract section of the PACK model. You want your prospects to realize they want to use your services. Many people think the word "sell" is a negative four-letter word. We see sell as positive. When you have something that you provide that creates value for other people, like your consulting services do, then it is only natural for you to want people to experience your services and benefit.

Think of it this way. Let's say you make amazing brownies. If you don't share them or tell other people about them, how can people enjoy them? Now you don't want to push them on people, right? You might want to say that you just made a batch of these terrific brownies and offer them up to people. It is up to the people you offer them to, to make the decision if they want one or not. They might not be hungry. They might be allergic to gluten. They may not like brownies. You don't need to do anything to convert people to eat your brownies other than produce them and make them available and let people know you have them if they want them.

This type of sell without selling approach really works and takes all the pressure off of you since you don't need to push or manipulate your prospects. You have probably purchased some goods or services where sales felt more like a tug of war. The sales person was pushing something on you and you were pulling back. Push and pull and pull and push—until either you walked away or purchased. That tug of war never feels good. So let's simply avoid using it.

LET THEM FEEL THEIR PAIN

Exactly how do you convert prospects without selling? It's really simple. You must show your prospective clients that they have a problem or problems in their business and have them actually feel the pain of that problem or problems if they continue not to have the problem(s) solved. Show and tell them what their issues are and use emotion to get them to wake up to the problem(s). Sometimes people try to avoid problems and your only role here is to show prospects that they have a problem and it's solvable. People hire business consultants to either remove a problem or move them to a goal.

Show prospects what you see as their gaps or problems or what is blocking them from achieving their business goals. Then, simply exhibit how you and your company can solve those problems and move them towards their goals. Clearly demonstrate to them that when they have your assistance in alleviating the issues, their business will perform better. Also help them to realize how much better they will feel with the problem(s) is resolved.

USING DIAGNOSTICS

We highly recommend revealing the problems to prospects by using some form of diagnostic assessment. You might call this a strategic assessment, or gap analysis, or business process evaluation, or even an initial consultation. It doesn't matter what term you use for this—the purpose is to use a short tool to see what gaps a business has and to then show the business your findings and how you and your company through your consulting expertise will remove the pain of the gap.

You can run a diagnostic on just about any area of a company from project management, sales force effectiveness, operations, HR, training and recruiting performance, supply chain management, process effectiveness, leadership, culture, and more. Your assessment helps the prospective client see the issues and helps you formulate strategies to remove their problems.

Your role during a diagnostic is to bring the elephant in the room, the real issue that is not being talked about, into focus and on the table. Think of it as sizing up the prospect's problem and then bringing awareness to their problem(s), and then creating solutions to remove the pain the problem(s) is (are) causing in the prospect's business.

The diagnostic can be very straight forward. You are simply assessing areas of the prospect's business to find any issues the company is having. This diagnostic will serve as the foundation of your consulting work and prospects will convert themselves into clients once you truly discuss the problems. This will provide the opportunity for you to share some of the solutions you bring to the table in the consulting project. Instead of selling, you are doing an analysis and then summarizing findings and being the professional consultant and not a salesperson.

Put yourself in the shoes of a prospective client for a moment. Before a prospective client brings in a consultant, they want to take a baby step to "try on" the consultant to be certain there is alignment. When a consultant does a diagnostic, the prospect is observing how the consultant works and thinks, and if that consultant actually fits with their organization.

An assessment or diagnostic tool is one of your most powerful instruments that allows you to move away from selling, and for the prospect to move into converting themselves as buyers of your consulting services. Through using assessments or diagnostics, you are bringing greater value to prospects without selling them, and you are revealing the prospect's problems and opening the prospect up to hiring your firm.

An effective business diagnostic will allow you to gain information about the business and then for you to identify, prescribe, and hopefully deliver effective remedies to address the gaps that showed up. You are able to be the solution to those areas where the company needs help. Imagine how this works. You conduct a diagnostic and show me, your prospective client, the elephant in the room. It's on the table in the open, and we all agree there is a problem or many problems. You may have dialed in on some issues the prospect did or did not know existed, and you have actually discovered the root causes of those issues. All that is left is for you to explain how your prospect's issues can be solved and the value that you will bring if they hire your firm. You must identify what you will be doing and, most importantly, the actual value they will receive either in terms of time saved or money created and/or saved, as well as other values like reducing frustration, improving morale, decreasing employee turnover, etc. Listen for the problems during the diagnostic and also for emotional triggers and frustrations. When you explain how you solve your prospect's problem(s), be certain to bring the emotional words into your conversation.

You might be wondering how the prospective client will convert themselves in this process. By conducting a diagnostic, you will be establishing your credibility, building rapport, and developing trust. When you are willing to bring up the prospect's problems, you engender confidence from them. When you show solutions, you are seen as the credible expert to the prospect. By asking insightful questions during the diagnostic, you are positioning yourself as the authority the prospect needs to assist with their business goals.

In addition to being seen as the credible expert, you must establish rapport with your prospective clients. The diagnostic serves as a way for you to get to know your prospects and show that you are interested in your potential clients as people. Through use of a diagnostic, you can get prospects to open up and to begin a relationship with them. Your prospects will also take notice of your listening skills. When you reflect back what you hear and ask clarifying questions, it becomes clear to prospective clients that you are relating to them. Acknowledging what prospects say without judgment and empathizing with them, allows prospects to gain greater rapport with you.

Credibility and rapport are keys to having prospects convert themselves into paying clients. During your diagnostic and review, demonstrate to the prospect you are sitting on their same side of the table and you are trying to determine what is best for the prospect and their business. This is how to sell without selling.

A successful diagnostic, where you have developed rapport and trust, will have you able to expose prospect problems, including some of the issues they might have been avoiding. It is very important that the prospect gets comfortable through this process and then can really see all the issues. Then they can decide if they want help solving their problems and seeing the big value in doing so.

AN ALTERNATIVE VIEW ABOUT PROPOSALS

Instead of selling, this consultative approach will have the prospect ask you to talk about how you work with them on a solution. Some consultants like to use actual proposals and some prospective clients will ask for proposals. A proposal is where you can put your recommendations for the client project on paper and you summarize your findings. Some consultants like to use these as they believe it makes them stand out and helps to convert prospects to become clients.

In Terri's business, she does not do proposals and also does not respond to Requests for Proposals (RFP's). Based on her business experience, responding to RFPs shaves her margin, dilutes her brand, and devalues her company position. The value of her business is to create differentiation for her company and not being lumped in with other consulting firms. Her role, as the business owner, is to conceive what the market doesn't know it needs. The RFP process allows the prospect to decide how she will do her work. She believes, "Great consultants lead their clients and we don't follow them." She won't spend the time to price and write out her consulting work in an RFP and then have a company take her intellectual property and select another firm to do the actual consulting work.

When asked for an RFP, she simply says, "Thank you for considering our company for your project." Then she states her company's Core Unique Positioning Statement, telling them, "if you want to discuss how our unique consulting services could benefit your project, I'd be delighted to meet with you." By using a quick template note or email, she either removes them from the radar or turns up a very serious prospect with this note or email.

When she was working as president of a national health company, they often sent out RFPs to gather intelligence that would help them decide if it was feasible to do the work internally. From the RFPs, they would have all the sources and information for a project that was never going to materialize. Learning from practices of that former employer, she prefers to discuss a diagnostic and then collaborate with the prospect to define the problem(s) and the solution(s). She believes this to be the fairest buying and conversion process. By sticking to her guns and refusing RFPs, she elevates her company's status in prospects minds.

Instead of an RFP, she sends the prospect one document that is her contract and describes the work her company will do clearly customized for them, based upon the findings and conversation from diagnostic work. During the diagnostic review, she discusses what the work will consist of and when her company would be starting the work, if the prospect selects her company. Then, in the contract, she summarizes the discussion and the dates to begin. If/when the prospect says "yes" and becomes a client, they are ready to go.

You may or may not decide to do RFPs. This is all up to you.

The biggest take-away from this section is meant to be how prospects convert themselves so you don't have to do traditional selling, by using a diagnostic or assessment.

Remember, for bonus resources
related to this chapter, go to:

www.TheUltimateGamePlanBook.com/resources

CHAPTER 10

• • • • • • •

KEEPING CLIENTS FOR THE LONG HAUL

MARKETING IS NOT JUST ABOUT acquiring new consulting engagements, it is also about how you keep clients long term. When you deliver value to your clients, and focus on continuing relationships with them, you can turn one-time clients into larger project engagements. Remember, marketing is retaining the clients you have and encouraging them to invest in your business consulting services repeatedly, for years. This is where the real profits are harvested in your consulting business.

Marketing boils down to understanding the three ways to grow any business:

1. Increase the number of customers
2. Increase the unit value of each purchase transaction
3. Increase the number of purchases each customer makes

It is more difficult and more expensive to find new clients than to market to your existing clients. Existing clients are your best prospects when you add on additional services because trust, credibility, and a relationship already exist. A client who is happy with the consulting services you have provided is your best prospect for your next related consulting service.

Business consultants who create a lot of repeat business are the ones who have thriving businesses. The best and biggest profits come from subsequent sales, beyond the client's initial consulting engagement. Your first engagement will have costs associated with client acquisition, but each subsequent engagement will have a higher percentage of built-in profit than the one before.

It is very important that you constantly enhance your value as a business consultant to your clients and build relationships where your clients feel that you have taken great care of them. This will lead to client renewals and client referrals.

KEEP IN TOUCH

Keeping in contact with current clients, former clients, and prospects is a skill set you must have. When we teach our Power Up systems for consultants and work with our mastermind clients, we show them how to put in place systems so that they can automate regular contact that might be of interest to prospects and clients. In our businesses we use tools like postcards, sales letters, and thank you cards. We also have a system to keep our prospects and clients up-to-date with any changes in our business such as new services and products.

We tell our mastermind clients that they want to be top of mind for their prospects and former and current clients—which means if and when prospects and clients need business consulting—your name comes to their minds first. Never forget that once you have a client, you need to work hard on their engagement and also work hard to build a long-lasting relationship with your clients to keep them.

This bears repeating: since the path to retaining a client starts with your performance in the current engagement that you have with them, you absolutely must always add tremendous value for every client that you serve. Clients must see that investing in your services was a great decision so that they think about you for every problem they have in the future. You want your clients to reflect on your great performance and the fantastic value they got from having you work with them on your very first engagement.

CLIENT INCENTIVES

Set up incentives right from your very early conversations with your potential clients. For example, during the proposal stage, you might propose that clients get implementation credit that they could use later in subsequent work for what they pay you to do now. One of the clients in our mastermind has his own proprietary diagnostic exercise. A client engaged him for a consulting project that was planned to last for two months and cost $100,000 in fees. This project included a great deal of analysis. However, it was not completed in the two-month period. The consultant wisely set up the client agreement so that the client could use a percentage of the initial consulting fee for future work.

Here's an idea: You can have a client use a percentage of the fees they paid in their first engagement toward other follow-on engagements. Clients don't want to lose this big discount and often will re-engage you so they can fully utilize the implementation credit. Just give an expiration period, such as "must be used during the next twelve months."

30,000-MILE CHECKUPS

After a client engagement has ended, we suggest to our mastermind clients that they schedule "30,000 mile checkups." This is the same concept that you have with your automobile maintenance program, where your auto dealer wants you to bring your car back in at various intervals on a maintenance program just for them to check under the hood and to make sure everything is okay. You can do the same thing with your clients. As part of the existing consulting contract, you schedule periodic checkups. The client will meet with you various time intervals for short visits to look under the hood. This way you are at the client's site and speaking with management decision makers. During these checkups, you and the company management will chat about problems and challenges the company is facing. Since you are on site, it will be the logical solution for you to solve the problems as they arise. If you were to lose contact with the client, the risk becomes you are out of sight and out of mind, and the client might not consider working with you to help solve their problems.

MONTHLY MEETINGS, QUARTERLY CHECK-INS, AND ANNUAL RETREATS

You can enhance your chances of getting re-hired when you hold structured meetings and reviews during the course of your engagement. In these meetings, you touch base with the executive decision makers about once a month to confirm that they do believe that the value you are bringing is always well worth their investment. The goal is always to show a return on investment for the client that exceeds the amount they invested for your services. Determine if there are any adjustments that need to be made or if the client sees issues or has questions about the value that they are receiving. By addressing these issues monthly, you will be able to ascertain if the client is pleased. You will also be able to assess if the client is experiencing a return on their investment which could lead to other work down the line with that same client.

We also suggest that you build ongoing coaching into your client agreements. By staying in the loop with your clients and being present for any issues or challenges they are having, you will be able to add value as you coach one or more executives or managers to most effectively implement the strategies that you have provided to them. Another way of maintaining some continuity with a client is by designing quarterly check-ins or an annual retreat. During these events, you will be providing some value added service. Services can range from being the client's keynote speaker at an event that they already have set up to doing a workshop that you design, manage, coordinate, and facilitate. Either way, the goal is to get you physically on site with the management team so you can stay abreast of their challenges and help them solve problems, while you're adding value physically in their presence.

CREATIVE NEGOTIATIONS

In the negotiating phase when you are crafting your client proposal, you might even be very creative and set up some of your compensation to include a percentage of the client's equity, or some other value based upon performance. This could be an equity percent or this could be a percent of revenue or profit gain that happens as a result of the work that you lead them through. You want to make sure that your strategies have long-term impact, and therefore incentivizes you to help maximize client results to become a win-win situation. Clients will be open to you coming back on site because ultimately they will get huge results in terms of increased revenue, reduced cost, higher cash flow—and they will make more money and also drive their stock price up. When you and the clients have the same goals of having a very successful engagement—and with you getting a piece of the pie based on the performance—optimum results can occur.

CREATING A MOVEMENT

Other ideas for client retention include getting your clients involved in some type of a movement. To create a movement, you may establish a community where your clients can participate and be active. You can set up communities through a Facebook group, a LinkedIn group, a Ming group, or a Google group. Once you establish this community, give members access to tools, resources, special information, and special events. You may even offer webinars or teleseminars. Give clients worksheets and templates to download as a member of the group. Have a focus so that people within the group are working towards the same goal or cause, like productivity or heartfelt leadership. Whatever it is, your clients become part of the movement with you, and it becomes a network where your clients are part of the process and become engaged. You can offer your group at no charge or you can charge a fee to belong. You can also do a blend, where you do allow members in for free, and if they want additional resources, they then pay a small fee. This community becomes an additional income resource, although this is not the real reason for establishing your group. The reason you really have the group is client retention. By keeping clients actively involved and engaged in the network, you raise the probability of maintaining consulting engagements.

WHAT'S NEW AND GOOD

Within your community you can reach out to clients by email, messaging, or phone calls. Offer new services. Introduce a new member of your team and the expertise they can deliver to the client that you did not have upon the time of the engagement. Or upsell a new service or product. We are not saying to create a product or service that a client does not need. You establish an upsell by looking to see how else you can add value to the client by adding more services to your repertoire. Whenever you do add services, be certain you inform your clients and offer those new services to them.

In addition to upselling, consider what you may be able to cross sell to your clients. Cross selling is offering additional services or products that will add value to your clients and is positioned along next to your consulting services. For example, one of our mastermind consulting client's business does not do assessments. However, she does offer them in her client engagements and has an arrangement to have another consultant who specializes in assessments deliver them to client organizations. Our client happily receives a nice percentage of every assessment the client's purchases.

SURVEYS

Start thinking about what offers you can add on to create even more value for your clients. "Begin with the end in mind" by focusing on the results you want your clients to have. Think about all the ways you can get clients even better results by adding products or services. To know which things your clients really want, we recommend you send out four-question surveys. These questions might be: What is your single biggest challenge at the moment? Are you meeting revenue goals? If not, what do you believe is the cause? Is there buy-in from employees on corporate or departmental changes?

These surveys will provide more information for you so that you better understand your client, and at the same time the clients will be telling you where they need help. Surveys are a great way to involve clients in the process. Whether it is through community or surveying, the whole intention is to establish long-term relationships and to engage the clients to speak back, answer back, and share their experience with you.

CONTENT DRIVEN EMAILS

We also suggest that you send your clients regular content-driven emails that include articles you have written, or audios you have recorded, or a link to a television show you appeared on, or a blog post you wrote, or just auto-responders with content. Send them regularly so you keep touching your clients. You want your clients to know that you care and that they matter.

SEND OUT CARDS

Additionally, we use a service called SendOutCards to keep in touch with our clients on a regular basis. This is an automated business tool that allows us to send out cards, set up campaigns, and personalize cards with the client's logo or a photo. This contact with clients keeps us fresh in their minds, and just might lead to additional contracts. If you want to try the system and to send a card out on our dime, just ask by emailing: info@businessconsultantinstitute.com

PICK UP THE PHONE

Frequently, we pick up the phone and randomly call some of our clients. We place an out of the blue call to clients when they are not expecting to hear from us at all, to let them know we thought of them that day, and wanted to check in. We might phone a client to share a really good idea with them, too. Clients really appreciate these calls and the calls let them know you are keeping them top of mind.

BLOGS, ARTICLES, AND MORE!

Remember, frequent blogging and article writing will keep you front and center for your audience—including your clients. Terri had one article that became very popular. It was titled "7 Ways to Overcome the Disengaged Employee." And since a disengaged workforce causes problems such as reduced productivity (meaning reduced profits) and high turnover, this spoke to a broad audience, some who were clients and likely to many potential prospects. Brainstorm topics that your clients need to know about. You can write articles for your own blog or even send articles out as press releases. Consider posting to group forums and larger news sites, such as *Huffington Post*. The more content that prospects and clients see, the more you are reinforcing the fact that they have come across or hired an expert who is an authority, and potentially even a celebrity. Hiring this type of consultant has long-term appeal. Prospects feel more secure in hiring you, and clients also are confident in continuing an ongoing relationship with you.

KNOW THE VALUE OF YOUR CLIENT

We teach our mastermind clients to always ask themselves: "What is this client worth to me?" Then we see how many dollars they are investing in marketing and how much time, energy, creativity, and money, it is actually costing them to land a client. Every client engagement has financial worth and you must also weigh client worth in other areas.

Many years ago, Terri had a nursing home come on board with her and the contract was worth $250,000 a year in consulting revenue. She believed that as she did a really good job for them, and when she met their needs, and even went above and beyond, they would realize she was engaged and would appreciate her touching base frequently. She trusted that the client would remain with her for about five years since that was the average time most clients remained on her roster. A $250,000-a-year client is nice. Even better is recognizing how much more the client was really worth when she multiplied five times $250,000. She realized what a huge financial asset this client was for her, and so she dedicated her company to adding even more value to the client engagement.

Terri shared a story with our mastermind clients to demonstrate how a business owner is not always focused on lifetime client worth. The client is a beauty salon owner who told Terri she closed the shop at 12 o'clock p.m. on Fridays. One week she became very upset because a prospective customer called at 11:45 a.m., saying that they were right around the corner and wanted to come in. The owner informed the potential customer that the shop was closing, that she was going to the beach, and that she couldn't see any other clients that day. The prospect was really angry. Terri asked the salon owner how much the first client visit brought into the shop. The salon owner said that the first client visit averaged $35, and then proceeded to tell Terri, somewhat defensively, this is why she did not keep the shop open because it was not worth it for a mere $35. Terri asked her if most clients come just once. The salon owner said that most clients have their haircut regularly. In fact, she said most of her clients visit every 6-8 weeks, and they stay twenty years—and they refer at least two family members. Do you see where this is going?

Terri then asked her to add up the value of the person that she would not take the time for because she was heading to the beach. Terri had her take that $35 across 6-8 weeks each year, and then multiply that over the course of twenty years, plus two more people like that as referrals from the client. When the salon owner did as Terri asked, she realized she had made a mistake that was far more than a $35 transaction! It was more like an $18,000 error, and possibly much more if the referrals kept on coming!

This is exactly why we tell all our mastermind clients that they must fully appreciate their clients. In our business, we think of our clients as our extended family and a client is anyone who buys any service or product. When you invest your first dime with us, we consider you our extended family. This is why we take our clients under our wings. We nurture them and always give them the results we promise and have a guarantee for our mastermind members. By creating massive value for your clients, they will remain with you long-term like ours do.

In every client conversation, you want to be mindful of the value the client has for you. Ensure that the client is happy with your performance so they will happily refer others to you and endorse you. We have multiple examples of clients who are now seven-figure relationships that began as five-figure or six-figure engagements. Although the client did not plan to be working with us over the next five years, we were able to solve their immediate problem in exchange for the consulting fee. And because they were happy with the results, they trusted us. Soon after, they understood the other capabilities that we possessed that could help them on an ongoing basis. Over the course of years, they became million-dollar clients. This can happen for you. We recommend to our mastermind clients that their objective be to serve the client so well that each client can become a million dollar one. No matter how small a contract might start out, we encourage you to think of every client as a million dollar client.

LEAD STRATEGY MEETINGS FOR YOUR CLIENT

Since you want to build long-term trust with your clients, we also recommend you become part of each client company's strategy meetings. A company's normal business cycle includes annual results of their financials with their budgets and bolted on to that process we recommend you suggest doing a strategy exercise to help them plan their next five years out, and to assist them in making decisions as they are doing so.

During these strategy meetings, facilitate conversations about what is happening in the marketplace, what customers want, what other suppliers are doing, and take a look at any markets or geographies that the company wants to enter. Your role is to help the company make decisions, line up for the future, set budgets, and make priorities for the next year. If you get yourself plugged into that exercise, and help your client to develop their strategies, this may lead to you getting a new engagement with the client that might be a strategy engagement or a strategy deployment process. Even if you do not get paid to facilitate this meeting, it may tie into something else you can do to serve the client so we recommend you suggest being a part of this for your clients.

Certainly, it is worth volunteering to facilitate a workshop for a couple of days to help clients with their budget and strategic planning. We have found that doing this has turned into many other opportunities for the folks we mentor in our mastermind and has led to more engagements for them and their teams.

Think about this: You are with the client in their planning and strategy process and have a first row seat to see their challenges and their strategies as well as to hear their aspirations. There is nothing more valuable than this insight. With it you will be able to assist executives in thinking through how they are going to handle these opportunities. If you happen to have capabilities on your team that line up with the challenges clients have and the strategies that they want to implement, then you have just increased your chances of being a partner in helping them to implement these strategies.

MORE ON CROSS SELLING AND UPSELLING

Earlier we discussed the concepts of cross sell and upsell. Our consulting teams possess a number of different skill sets that determine how we work with clients. For example, Pete's consulting company includes all types of business transformation such as leadership development work, culture shifting, operational improvement methods, using Lean and Six Sigma concepts, their proprietary strategic goals deployment process, defining company strategies, and getting employees aligned with those strategies to make sure everyone is focused on the right initiatives, and aligning the company's purpose, vision, mission, and goals. All of these areas come together and have a role in the long-term success for a business. Ideally, a company would hire them for a full business transformation over the next five years. What actually happens is Pete's company is hired to solve a specific problem or help in one of the above areas. It might be to execute strategy, diagnose operational challenges, or define a more desirable culture. Once that specific project is complete, there will likely be other conversations about problems in other areas where the client needs assistance. Eventually, the discussion might be about the complete business transformation. See how this works?

You will actually start with consulting projects and specific initiatives in all of the areas that you, as a consulting team, have skill and expertise. It would be great to get five-year engagements right out of the gate where you could help every company maximize results over that period of time.

The reality is that consulting does not work this way. Instead, you will get hired for a very specific problem that you may be asked to solve. Then from that very specific problem, because of your performance demonstrating your problem-solving skills and strategic thinking in other areas, companies ask you to do more. For example, they may ask you to add operational diagnostic exercises to help the executive team understand the level of performance they should be getting out of their operations and help them itemize what needs to get done for them to achieve the level of results they desire. In such a case, you would pick up a narrow business transformation. In other instances, you might expand the consulting agreement with the client engaging you for the full scope of your services.

Terri shares the example of getting hired to help a sales team improve their results. Her company was then asked to assist with leadership training, hiring practices, and to work on marketing processes and systems, as well.

No matter where you begin with a client, recognize that you always have the opportunity to expand the conversation to talk about some more of what you do. Maybe you will be able to discuss leadership elements that are needed once you are in the company and see that need. Perhaps you will see cultural dynamics that are in place and be able to suggest some areas where you can assist with strategies by pointing out how you are actually observing misalignments of what people are working on and how this is holding the company back. Share your real observations and talk about themes of what you see in this company and then bring up intellectual content telling the client what you have done in the past with other similar companies or organizations.

We suggest you write out case studies of other clients as a way to add extra value and demonstrate that there are a number of other ways that your consulting skills can help clients achieve their goals. They may not know to ask for the additional things your company is capable of bringing to them and may not recognize they have gaps in other areas that you have not addressed. Always guide client conversations to help them solve their challenges and *always* add value all along the way.

HERE'S HOW IT WORKS FOR US

In our consulting businesses, we often find we get hired for a diagnostic engagement that then leads to a series of engagements. One diagnostic can turn into a culture shifting engagement, and then this turns into a strategy setting and strategic-goal deployment engagement, and more, depending on what else comes up in the client's business. Remember, every business is dynamic. Problems that clients have today will change as the year goes on. Surprises will pop up in their day-to-day business. You may be on site with a client when suddenly there is a big supplier quality issue, and you happen to know something about how to solve that supplier quality issue. Or, you can jump in and teach sales strategies to help with the customer crisis your client is experiencing. You can then suggest that you design that solution for them—in addition to the work you are already doing. This is how your consulting engagements keep expanding.

CONSULTING BUSINESS PROCESS

As with all businesses or projects, there is a process, and these are the steps we've identified for the consulting business:

1. Discover the client's need or problem.

2. Communicate a better way and describe the potential value to your client.

3. Propose the project.

4. Sign a contract.

5. Execute the project.

6. Invoice your client and receive payment.

7. Ask for referrals and testimonials.

8. Repeat (for this client or other clients).

Start with your client. Get them to the solution they need. Let them know what else you do. *Yes, it is as simple as that!*

**Remember, for bonus resources
related to this chapter, go to:**

www.TheUltimateGamePlanBook.com/resources

SECTION V

• • • • • • •

DELIVERING AWESOME VALUE

We've established that delivering awesome value to your client in every engagement is critical.

In this section, we discuss what you need to put in place to help you deliver the highest value possible. In part that means you need to commit to be a lifelong learner. Developing your consulting skills so that you can maximize your effectiveness in the consulting engagements is a continuous process. In Chapters 11 and 12, we've outlined some of the top skills that you need including problem solving, coaching skills and leadership capabilities.

In Chapters 13 and 14, we also introduce what we call the *Maximum Client Impact Model,* which describes many specific elements of your consulting method, including details of managing your consulting engagements and the interactions with your client team members that will maximize your impact and the value you deliver. We outline the processes to have in place and be set up for success before you launch your project and also processes necessary to rely upon during your engagement.

CHAPTER 11

· · · · · · ·

DEVELOP YOUR CONSULTING SKILLS

WE SHARE WITH OUR MASTERMIND clients that to be the most successful consultants possible they must bring great value to every consulting project. If you want to be in demand and command high fees, we know that you need to start with your own skill building. One reason consultants join our mastermind is that they have decided to be relentless in their ongoing skill building and want to widen their breadth of knowledge and expertise.

If a business owner is going to engage with a consultant, they want to entrust their business to a business consultant who has a high level of expertise in the specific topic area they are seeking help in. In *Outliers: The Story of Success*, Malcolm Gladwell makes the case that experts have 10,000 hours of experience with the topic they claim as their expertise. He suggests that our genius isn't just a given if we have a knack for it. We must develop a practice to get better in whatever area we want to achieve success.

Similarly, Cal Newport, author of *So Good They Can't Ignore You,* suggests that deliberate practice is in order, meaning we must continually stretch ourselves beyond our comfort zone.

"To get better—and win the promotions and opportunities most of us dream about—we must set out to intentionally improve our performance. Most knowledge workers inadvertently end up avoiding deliberate practice-style activities because they retreat to checking email the moment a task gets too difficult. To make deliberate practice work, you must not only tolerate unpleasantness (and stick with the task, regardless of your urge for relieving distraction), but learn to seek it, like a bodybuilder seeks muscle burn," he writes in *The Wall Street Journal* article, "Want that Promotion, Practice Your Job."

Using a forty-hour-work week as a measure, this means you would need five years of full-time experience in your area of expertise. But that means focused time on your specific area. If you are a generalist consultant and you spread your time across four disciplines, then you would need four times that five years or twenty equivalent years of experience to adequately reach expert status. The reality is, a true expert is not punching the clock for a forty-hour week. Rather, they are passionate about their topic and immerse themselves in reading, studying, researching, and practicing every available minute. They truly become an expert very rapidly.

We are adamant about continuous skill development for ourselves and for our mastermind clients because there will be inevitable speed bumps along the way while you are serving clients and those skills will help you quickly continue rolling along again. Frequently, it is not enough to simply have a business plan, you also need to constantly work on your own business model design and have your own mission and vision statements, as well as shift your offerings, your pricing, and profit models. Be certain you are setting aside money for your own business consulting and mentoring so you constantly obtain the skills and knowledge you need. We practice what we teach here, and regularly invest in mentors ourselves. You should, too.

If you do not have business coaching skills, you need to learn these. Business consultants work with human beings who have their own set of strengths and weaknesses. Coaching skills—tuning in and deeply listening, asking powerful questions, communicating to seek clarity and to provide focus—are essential. You also want to learn coaching skills of growing and building clients—and holding clients accountable for implementing actions and dealing with difficult situations.

Be certain to truly understand your niche—and what their more difficult challenges are. (See Section VI). Know the topic areas where you really are an expert, where you've practiced for those 10,000 hours we referenced earlier, or if you need to bring on team members to assist you. Once you identify your niche—your ideal audience—you want to take time to learn the problems that most prospects in that niche have and then formulate a strategy to define and solve those problems. You may even need or want to develop your own proprietary strategies or tools and establish your own consulting toolkit.

We find in our work with our mastermind clients that they need skill development in systematizing their businesses for maximum efficiency. You may need assistance to develop templates, automation, and sales scripts. Most of our clients also need skill development in marketing and creating marketing systems, as well.

We have been talking about developing your skills related to business. Let us not forget that skill development always includes personal development. Our mastermind clients are usually surprised when we have an opportunity to coach them on their blocks, weaknesses, and other life issues that get in the way of their success. You must continually be working on your own personal skills and improving them, just as we work on ours and improve these skills for our clients in our mastermind, also.

And we practice what we preach. We believe that learning from masters helps us earn more. We have both invested in mentors and consultants to help learn problem solving, decision-making, project management, and time-management skills. These four skills typically are needed for you to run your own consulting business more successfully and is also what clients require to enhance the success of their business.

LEARN FROM MASTER CONSULTANTS

You may be surprised at all the roles you play and hats you wear running your own consulting business. Accept the fact that you won't know all you need to know about marketing, accounting, e-commerce, managing employees and/or independent contractors, and hiring the right ones and training them properly. And that's okay. What's important is knowing where to turn for assistance—and doing so in a timely manner before a crisis erupts. Nothing will derail success more than having to put out fires—and ones that could be avoidable.

Instead of reinventing the wheel, discover savvy shortcuts by hiring leading consultants to be your mentors and to help you run your business and market your business more successfully. If you are just starting a consulting business, or if you are already a business consultant, realize that it takes more than a business card and some organizational ability to make a great deal of money and to have long-term success as a business consultant. There will be hurdles. Having someone in your corner who has *been there-done that* when you meet these obstacles can quickly get you through the challenges.

Some of our clients need help getting comfortable with sales and selling themselves. Others need help finding the right contacts, pricing, what fee structure to use, creating their business plan and then following that plan. Then there are those who require assistance in deciding what type of entity to establish for their business—a sole proprietorship, a partnership, a limited corporation, an S Corporation. Some even need help selecting a business and domain name while others want assistance with errors and omissions insurance, positioning, branding, entering new markets, content for their website, setting up their social media presence, and then using social media as a form of reverse marketing.

We have worked with mastermind clients who needed to get leads quickly and assistance in effectively networking. Then there were those who are in start-up mode and others who are super profitable and want to work fewer hours. Others have had a long meaningful career and want help selling their consulting businesses.

One of the biggest challenges for our mastermind clients is developing skills in keeping the cash flow steady and reliable. You have to know how much cash you need to keep your business going. Most businesses fail because they don't have enough cash to fund daily operations so we make certain our clients build their cash.

As you market yourself as a business consultant, you clearly must be able to perform the work that a business consultant does. It's necessary to learn skills and apply the ones you develop so you can have high impact on your clients. How you apply business consulting skills and execute those skills will determine not only your success but also the success your clients have in achieving their goals.

In the remainder of this chapter we review the top, "must have" skills for consultants: problem solving, coaching, synthesizing, communicating, and listening.

PROBLEM SOLVING

The crux of consulting is solving problems for clients, and so you need to be a great problem solver. Problem solving is critical to consulting because you are there presumably because your client has some problems that they need to solve. Client problems can be lack of revenue, lack of customers, organizational issues, profit issues, systems issues, supply chain issues, employee challenges, growth and diversification, or anything that is in their way of achieving their strategic business goals. The problem might even be not having a viable strategy in the first place! There will also be certain challenges that the companies and organizations you work with will need to tackle along the way, within or along side of the work you are hired to do.

There are multiple dimensions to problem solving including the analytic skills to review data such as financial statements, spreadsheets, and reports of various areas like customer data, human resources reports, inventory reports, output in production reports, etc. You will also collect your own data or design data sheets for your client to collect when what you really want to know isn't readily available in a report. You might tap into your inner spreadsheet guru to look at data from a variety of perspectives. You'll need to dive deep into data to pull out patterns and understand what the data is saying so you can draw some conclusions.

Good problem solving starts with a hypothesis and then testing the hypothesis much like a scientist would help you be efficient in whatever it is that you are studying. To get you started, talk to your client to learn what they think the problem is. Set up interviews to hear everyone's points of view. You will find interviewing is sometimes like the story of a blind man discovering an elephant: if he touches the tail, he describes an elephant to be like a rope. If he touches the leg, he describes it to be like a tree. If he touches its side, he describes the elephant to be like a wall. You'll need to assemble the collective points of view into the full picture. It is a good idea to have the financial and operational metrics to review as well, so that you can match what you are hearing in your discussions with how the company is measuring its performance. You can form your hypotheses based on these collective inputs.

Then it is necessary to very quickly draw some preliminary conclusions so that you can move fast from problem to preliminary answer, to testing, to see if you are accurate in the answers. Once you are certain you understand the root causes and have defined strategies to implement, make sure the client is capable of implementing them. Your client might ask for help or might go forward without you. Either way, the problem isn't solved until the solutions are implemented and sustained over time. If you're engaged for support beyond the initial diagnostic phase, recognize there are many factors that could prevent the problem solving from reaching its conclusion. You need to stay ahead of the client and keep them from giving up too quickly so that results don't slide back.

Within the problem-solving arena, having a structured thought process is very important. This structured thought process gives you the hypothesis based problem-solving structure. This provides some standardization in your consulting. This type of thought process will help when you have multiple people on your consulting team in a client engagement. If you add team members to your consulting business, make sure they have the exact problem-solving skills that you have as this is a must in moving clients forward.

Commit to improving your problem solving skills. We could write an entire book about the problem solving process because it is so important for your success as a business consultant. In fact, the large consulting firms invest weeks training their consultants in problem solving. When Pete was at McKinsey and Company he had three weeks of intense training during his first two years at the firm, and problem solving was a core element of that curriculum. It really is that important.

COACHING

One of the tools in a consultant's tool kit can also be coaching, which is a form of consulting, and is really effective in assisting to identify client problems so that you can solve their problem. Again, the difference between coaching and consulting is in coaching you are asking the client to come up with their own answers using introspective coaching questions and skills like the use of powerful requests, powerful questions, and powerful observations. (See more on consulting versus coaching in Chapter 17.)

These coaching tools can help unearth what the problems truly are that clients are facing. When you ask a client a powerful coaching question, it basically stops them in their tracks and makes them think about something they never thought about before. A few examples would be:

* If I were to give you an extra hour a day, what would you do with it?

* What would you do if you had unlimited resources?

* What story is holding you back?

* What will you do first?

* How much energy are you willing to put into that?

* How would your ideal self create a solution?

* If I was in your shoes and asked for advice, what would be the first thing you'd tell me?

* What would you try now if you knew you could not fail?

* Just because that happened in the past, why must it happen again?

* Is what you are doing helping you follow your joy?

* What is the experience you are looking to create?

* How does this decision match up with who you know you are?

* When will you start?

* What small steps can you take to get you closer to your vision?

* What are you waiting for?

* What do you think the moral of that story is?

* What part of what you've just said could be an assumption?

* What are the positive outcomes of this negative situation?

* What story do you most often hear yourself telling?

* What am I not asking you that you really want me to ask?

A powerful request can also stop your client and have them really think about what you are asking them. In our experience, powerful requests unearth a very difficult problem that clients are dealing with. To make a powerful request:

* Stay connected to what you care about. Don't let superfluous details cloud the request and as you lead in to the request, keep what you care about firmly in mind.

* Be truly open to yes, no, or counter offer. If you cannot stomach a "no" or counter offer, you're not making a request; you are delivering a demand.

* Make the lead-in short. No sob stories, no long explanations. Big wind-ups often transfer your emotional burden onto the person of your request intentions. That's compulsion, not a powerful request. So, state just enough to give context for the request and then say, "I request..." This is the power of a powerful request. Simply, "I request you refund me the room rate..." "I request you take out the trash..." "I request you help me understand what you really need..." "I request you meet with me today to finish the marketing brochure..."

That's it. Simple, and effective.

Using the skill of powerful observation can even drive home what you are seeing about the problem and have the client go under the layers just a little bit deeper.

When it comes to observation, especially today, we must get more tactical and prescriptive in our coaching as opposed to offering more generic and hollow advice. Managers need to observe exactly what their people are doing in the field or operation, during a presentation, during a cold call, and when managing an account.

Interestingly, observation is clearly one of the most critical responsibilities managers seem to be avoiding most and ironically the one that yields the greatest return regarding the payoff they'll experience in relation to their time invested. You can add a ton of value by making the observations and also teaching the skill to your client.

So, why is there such resistance around engaging in this activity? While managers may complain that they "don't have the time for this," the real cause of their reluctance has to do with the fact that they feel observation is really hard, even confrontational and uncomfortable at times. This is only difficult because most managers have never been shown how to do this correctly. The result: most simply don't do it, and if they do, it's more toxic than helpful.

In truth, managers are really not paying attention. When a manager is observing their people, much of the time they're already viewing what they see in their mind's eye, what they perceive is the right way and in turn, that's what they're listening for. In other words, they're seeing how that person is not modeling the way they do it, and they are rigid in the way they want it done.

As a result, the manager winds up coaching to their own image rather than uncovering and co-creating new possibilities and identifying what is best for that person—all due to the rigidity in their thinking.

For example, when observing one of their salespeople make a cold call, after the person hangs up the phone, the manager is overheard saying:

* Here's what you did wrong.

* Why didn't you do it this way?

A more effective dialogue might begin with other questions such as:

* What were your goals for that call?

* How do you think that call went? Did you meet the goals?

* What could you do next time to make the call more effective?

* When do you speak with the client next?

Additional coaching skills include: exploring the truth, challenging the client, holding a bigger vision, and a lot more.

As a consultant, you may have to create a sense of urgency with some of the leadership or team members to move your engagements along—and that may require having some conversations, pointing out what others may not be willing to admit aloud themselves. This is not intended to be shaming or hurtful, but supportive, to provide feedback that allows your clients or their team members to dissolve barriers to success.

When delivering a successful truth conversation, be mindful of the tone of your voice and be sure to exhibit empathy for the individual on the receiving end of your feedback. Be specific in your observations and from there create goals to establish new behaviors that will ensure the success of the individual and the client's overall mission.

And as always, allow the individual to have an opportunity to respond to your observations—and to come up with their own action plan. Frequently, we need a little space between receiving feedback and devising ways to change our behaviors. By giving the individual this chance, they'll buy into any modifications in their approach to their responsibilities and won't feel coerced to accept someone else's plan.

If they feel like a teenager forced to go along on summer vacation with the family, you might observe some resistance. Defensive behaviors will often arise if the feedback is delivered with an iron fist. While being firm is important, remember presentation is everything.

Core coaching skills also assist in the problem-solving equation and will get the client problems on the table. These coaching skills are critically important as part of your interaction with your clients and when you are interviewing various members of the client's team to find out their perspectives of the problems, their perspectives of the issues and challenges, and frankly, how things work on a day-to-day basis. During interviews with the client and their employees, you will be asking questions and inquiring for data so you can actually see the issues with your own eyes as opposed to sitting in a conference room or at a desk.

SYNTHESIZING

At the end of your problem solving process, you then need to draw your conclusions by synthesizing what you learned. Synthesize means to combine a number of things into a coherent whole.

Synthesis is a skill that is different than summarizing because you are extracting the meaning beyond simply creating the executive summary of what you found. Here, you draw conclusions and as you synthesize those conclusions, this will then lead to the actions that are required and the recommendations that you make back to the client. The bulk of consulting is truly identifying the problems that the client has and then working with your clients to solve those problems. Solving client problems is the benefit and the result of all client engagements. How well you solve problems will determine client satisfaction, client referrals, and long-term project engagements.

COMMUNICATING

As we all know, communication comes in both verbal and written forms, as well as body language—and requires one to be highly adept in using all of them. Both verbal and written communications have a variety of subsets. Verbal communication includes everything from one-on-one conversations, interviewing, giving presentations in front of a room, leading training, and perhaps highlighting a meeting where there is a group of people around the conference room table or a team of people in a stand up meeting in front of a visual board. Written communication includes emails, proposals, letters, and contracts. Having your written recommendations summarized and itemized in a program like PowerPoint or a Word document—and available to your team—is a great asset. As a business consultant, you have to express your findings and recommendations in words and graphics in such a way that you get your point across—and are moving the client to action—with as much communication as is required and with as few words as you can get away with to deliver the message. Communication is clearly an art form that you will develop over time. It's a practice.

When you have good command of the language, there is clarity in how you communicate with your clients. You are not hampering how people hear what you are saying. There are ways to communicate that are most effective, yet sometimes in our communications, we do not realize our roadblocks. We might be using words like "should" or "ought to"—otherwise known as "stop" words. We may accidentally criticize, blame, or probe too much. While probing is necessary in our business, excessive probing can cause distrust between the client and ourselves. When the client becomes sensitive to our questioning, they may not want to communicate with us. And if that is the case, then we are not able to perform our jobs and fulfill our contracts—or even land a contract in the first place.

Another part of communication is body language. Communication goes beyond words and tone. Nonverbal cues are often more important than spoken words. Be sure to look directly at your client when speaking, avoid crossing your arms, and put the technology away. Give your client your complete attention—and take cues from their body language, which is a skill of active listening.

LISTENING

Listening is vital to any relationship. We need to be able to deeply tune in to what is being said by our clients and also what is underneath the words the client is saying to us. As we listen, we must give our clients undivided attention, listen for underlying feelings, and notice any keywords that client is using. It is our responsibility to avoid prejudging the value of spoken words. Instead of thinking about what we are going to say and formulating our consulting advice, we have to really hear what our clients are saying. It's important to allow our clients to complete all their thoughts and communicate in turn.

Be careful when you are communicating with clients that you do not always have the last word, one-upping the client and showing your expert status. Your clients must feel like they are a winner in the communication. As you are listening to your clients, make a conscious effort to consider the logic of what the client is saying and whether or not it is valid and credible. You want to listen in an objective way being *charge neutral*. This means you listen with no attachment to the outcome. Forget about thinking of "I, I, I, I, I, I," and how you feel. Instead, comment back to your client from a place of neutrality. When you speak in a charge neutral tone, you are speaking in the same way just as you would say, "Would you like a cup a coffee?" You would have no agenda in offering coffee. Charge neutral talk means zero agenda or attachment to any outcome that proves your knowledge and coddles your ego. You would not have any agenda asking if the client wanted coffee. Nor should you have any agenda when asking anything of the client.

Also, you always want to check in with the client, to ensure mutual understanding. One way you can do this is to ask, "Is that right?" or "Did I understand?" Do this check-in frequently and make a very conscious effort to be certain you are on the same page and do not take communication for granted. Clarification statements are very important for full communication to occur.

All of these are skills of active listening. Techniques such as paraphrasing what you heard and double-checking the quality of the information you heard both verbally and nonverbally play a very significant role, too. Only seven percent of what is being said comes across with words. Twenty-three percent of what is being said is understood through tone of voice. Most important-ly, thirty-five percent of what is said is communicated through facial expressions and another thirty-five percent through body language. This all means that when you are actively listening, you want to pay deep attention to the speaker's words while perceiving their tone of voice, as well as their facial and body expression. Active listening doesn't mean you agree with the speaker, however. It means you hear and understand.

Although you might not possess all of these advanced commu-nication skills right out of the gate, you can polish them. You have enough skills to get started today. Like all of the consultants we work with in our mastermind, you will learn from your mistakes and your opportunities. The more that you are in front of clients, the better you will become. When you work with the right coach-es and get mentoring from skilled consultants for your consulting business, you will learn faster and earn more. And again, as con-sultants, we must practice what we preach. Seek the knowledge you need to take your business to the next level.

Another advanced skill related to communication includes knowing when to "poke the client in the eye." This is a phrase that means just as you would poke a bear with a stick, so it would wake up and chase you, you need to nudge clients to get them to move. If you do it in the wrong way, they will eat you.

One thing you want to be aware of is what we refer to as "call-ing the baby ugly." Imagine that you happen to be with a client who created a process and it is broken. The client may resist your recommendations to change, and they may resist your data and acceptance that proves their process is broken. Being able to communicate the reality and the truth of the situation in a way that is fact based and clear helps the client to gain acceptance of your observations and ideas. Do your best to take emotion out of your communication and stick with facts and data. When it is your opinion, be clear what your opinion is and why you have that opinion.

COMMON LISTENING ERRORS

One listening error is when you *overanalyze*. Here, you are constantly interpreting and trying to understand the underlying motives of what the client is saying. Instead, take in what the client is saying without having an agenda for analyzing.

Be aware of the listening error called *lagging*. Lagging is where you are mentally backtracking to something you have heard and are not being fully present to the client.

Omitting is another error, similar to lagging, when you only catch part of what the client says, hook on to that piece, and then you miss what is actually underneath those words.

Undershooting is common when you are not really understanding your client's feelings, and you are only listening to their words—and perhaps missing the tone of their voice, and even their expression. When you do this, you will miss the value of what is really being said by your client.

Overshooting is when you intensify the emotions that you hear, and instead of listening beyond the words and emotions by trying to grasp what the client is saying, you might accidentally be feeling more intensity in their words.

Avoid *rushing* the client along to finish what they want to say and do not use phrases such as "I know," "I have been there," "I get it," "I hear you." Sit quietly and do not interrupt with phrases like these. It's good to be empathetic, but only when it's genuine.

Frequently, a very common listening error is *adding*. Here, you begin to generalize what a client says and you add to what the client has said.

And perhaps the worst (or most annoying) of all—some consultants confuse *parroting* or *mirroring back* as a skill set. You never want to take someone's exact words and constantly use them back to them. When you engage in this communication behavior, it can be taken as an insult to repeat something back to the person. We find it shocking that mirroring is a skill taught in a lot of coaching textbooks.

Remember your role is to be a listener, and as a listener, you are really an observer asking directional and clarifying questions—and not jumping to the analysis of the problem. As a listener and a great communicator, before you give any ideas or solutions be certain to ask your client's permission first. When we listen to our clients in our consulting engagements, we are always very attentive. We look for the non-verbal cues and are very interested in what our clients are saying both verbally and nonverbally. Our role is to be the summarizer, collaborating with the speaker to identify what their problem areas might be, and then going into problem-solving mode after we have done a good job of listening.

**Remember, for bonus resources
related to this chapter, go to:**

www.TheUltimateGamePlanBook.com/resources

CHAPTER 12

* * * * * * *

ADVANCED SKILL DEVELOPMENT

IN THIS CHAPTER WE CONTINUE to describe some important skills for you to develop. As you continue to work with new clients, refer back to this chapter and consciously practice the skills we list here for you.

MODEL LEADERSHIP

Leadership is an essential skill for all consultants. There are three levels of leadership: self-leadership, team leadership, and client leadership. Self-leadership is important because you, as the individual, need to be modeling leadership behavior. You play the role of the leader that you want your team and your clients to see and emulate. Always remember that as the leader, all eyes will be on you because you are the paid expert who is helping the client out. If you have a team of resources working with you as your consulting team, they are also (hopefully) modeling you because it is your team that you are leading. This is where interpersonal skills and traditional soft skills come into play. The team dynamics, the communication, the leadership skills you have all enhance the harmony that ensures that your consulting engagements go smoothly and yield great client and team results.

You must be good at self-management so that you can have a high level of efficiency and productivity as a consultant. Self-management is important for two reasons: The first is that client engagements tend to be high paced with high levels of expectations. You need to create a lot of impact and complete a lot of work in a very short period of time for your clients. It is crucial that you churn out that work efficiently. Secondly, again because all eyes are on you, if you appear to be organized and productive, the client's perception will be that they are getting their value from what it is you are doing and delivering. The truth is the real value actually comes from the bottom line results that you achieve for your clients. If their financials change because of your involvement, and they see bottom line impact, then they will be happy and believe your consulting has made a true difference for their company.

However, along the way, what they see with their eyes matters a lot, and they will perceive you to be adding value or not adding value, independent of how their financials change, by what they observe. It is essential that you are highly organized, productive, and efficient in how you run meetings, excel at your presentations, and display high level communication skills. Self-leadership will make a very big impact on your clients and your consulting team.

LEADING VERSUS MANAGING

In our view, traditional managing is truly dead. We have seen that the command and control model does not work and is one of the reasons why those companies who have relied on this method have lost a lot of business. Companies began to use the command and control model in World War I, placing employees in the position of having to obey as children being told what to do, rather than be empowered to own responsibility for their roles. Instead of being a commander or controller, you want to be certain that you are modeling a leadership position versus a manager position. And then take it a step further by doing both.

There is a saying that "Managers do things right, while leaders do the right thing." Peter Drucker, known as the "inventor of modern management," and one who saw business as a human-driven enterprise that could be profitable *and* socially responsible, believed that good leadership is a synthesis of both—doing the right thing while doing things right. The trick is in taking action with integrity and having respect for those you work with. If you do that, then you will not only move your projects forward with right action, but you will also be doing what's right for the people involved.

DEVELOP YOUR INTUITION

Sometimes knowing what is right requires that you use more than just your five senses. A key to leadership success is the use of our intuition and that requires a great deal of self-awareness and non-attachment.

While you may be hands-on with your five senses and don't fully believe in your intuition or sixth sense, we're betting that you rely on your intuition much more than you realize. In fact, in the Myers Briggs Type Indicator, Sensing versus Intuition is one of the four pairs of preferences or dichotomies that the tool measures.

Whether your preference is to acknowledge that you use your intuition or not, you can learn to develop a stronger trust of your intuition and increase the quality of your leadership. One way is to view situations with neutrality. Make sure you are in a good mood when you tap into a situation. See if your ideas and plans bring you joy, worry, fear, or doubt. The best way to remain neutral is to stay in the present moment. If you feel triggered by a situation, you are likely reacting to a present moment situation based on emotions from a past experience.

Developing your intuition requires slowing down and allowing space for inspiration to find you. The biggest destroyer of intuition is your busy schedule. Begin a practice of unplugging yourself from your tasks and technology on a daily basis, preferably at the same time each day. Whether you call this meditation, contemplation, or just chill time, it's essential for inviting those "eureka" or "aha" moments into our consciousness.

Be sure to acknowledge those times when you've had sense about something, followed it, and the results validated your "hunch." This will set the stage to become more intuitive on more occasions.

BE EMOTIONALLY INTELLIGENT

As a leader, you also want to make sure you are celebrating successes and achievements no matter how small they might be. All truly good leaders always give praise to others, do not take all of the recognition, and are observant. We find one of the highest leadership qualities is to understand inspiration and to be able to lead with genuine excitement. You want to be a passionate leader who is self-leading. Self-leading means you show up at client engagements in a driven way, and you are excited to get to the goal, to be part of the client team. Make sure you are taking the steps that you need to be inspired. Use emotional intelligence skills such as self-awareness, self-discipline, persistence, empathy, excitement, and passion about the client engagement to drive results. Pay attention to the negative emotions so they do not affect your decision-making skills.

Great leaders manage their emotions, especially the ones that we call the big three—anger, anxiety, and sadness. These are normal human emotions and you are a human being who is going to experience these emotions. Yet, it's important not to let them rule the helm. As a leader, remember that you are not only motivating other people, you are also motivating yourself. The root of the word motivation is the Latin word move. As a leader you are moving other people, and you also want to move yourself. Keeping your emotions in check is necessary for staying in motion. Unresolved issues can lead to habits of procrastination—and in some cases depression.

The important thing for you to realize is that your emotions are real and they're important indicators. Again, if we were working with you in person, as one of our individual clients or as part of our mastermind, we might tailor this discussion more specifically to your situation and use coaching skills to lead you to a greater degree of self-discovery about your feelings and why they are occurring. Just remember, being self-aware of how you're feeling and *why* is vital. You cannot read other people's emotions, unless you are really tapped into and in-tune with your own emotions.

According to Brent Gleeson, Navy Seal veteran and author of *From the Battlefield to the Board Room*, "A leader lacking in emotional intelligence is not able to effectively gauge the needs, wants and expectations of those they lead. Leaders who react from their emotions without filtering them can create mistrust amongst their staff and can seriously jeopardize their working relationships. Reacting with erratic emotions can be detrimental to overall culture, attitudes, and positive feelings toward the company and the mission. Good leaders must be self-aware and understand how their verbal and non-verbal communication can affect the team."[1]

A leader has the skill of enhancing productivity and continuous growth in an organization or a company—whether your clients' or your own. Make sure you are constantly motivating the client (and your team) and driving toward an end result as efficiently as you can. Further, you have to make sure that you are demonstrating your core values as the consultant or consulting company when you have multiple people on your client teams. Develop your team and their skills right alongside your own. Be the leader and watch your team and your client follow.

Be certain to notice how you are managing and leading yourself all the time. Take responsibility for your own self-management and emotional behaviors. Always remember what we said earlier—the leader is followed and the manager rules. Be a leader.

GIVE AND RECEIVE FEEDBACK

When you are managing a team in an organization, you want your team members to have very specific behaviors. One mandatory behavior is that your team be able to give constructive feedback, and to make sure that feedback is always motivational. Many times feedback may need to be given to you.

---

1 "The Use of Emotional Intelligence for Effective Leadership" Forbes, DEC 29, 2014

You will want to foster the ability to receive feedback—particularly when things aren't going as well as you had hoped. In these situations, it's important to own up to your errors and then create the space for your team to offer their feedback. A leader makes other people feel right, respected, and valued.

Every good leader will come face-to-face with difficult situations from time to time, and they must have the ability to make really tough decisions. They know by making these decisions they move an organization forward. Leaders who have a team also know how to facilitate positive interactions amongst the team to keep the momentum. Members may have very different personalities and a leader focuses on keeping an organization stable—particularly amidst change. A good leader has vision and holds that vision for the organization—and is the one that gets everybody rallied around that vision. A part of leading a team is the ability to promote adaptability, and at the same time, stability, within an organization. Influence is about communicating at the highest level. And that includes offering valuable feedback every step of the way.

MANAGE CLIENT EXPECTATIONS

For client leadership, some of the important things to call attention to include managing the client's expectations and making sure the project that you are overseeing has a specific set of deliverables and is on track. It is vital that the client understands the status and is doing their part to ensure a successful project. What sometimes happens in a client situation is that a client thinks that magically you, the consultant, will make everything happen for the company and the resources on the client's side are too busy to complete assignments. This may include finding dates for having conversations or implementing certain tasks. When these actions do not happen according to the timeline that you expect, the project may slip. Then the project can be at risk for delivering the results that you promised. Client leadership includes status checks and update meetings to make sure clients and team members are able to deliver what you are asking them to on time and in good order.

Feedback isn't always "positive." Frequently, your clients may need to receive feedback that their own behavior, or that of the team, is creating obstacles to project fulfillment. One of the other things to take into account is making sure any feedback that you are giving is not a criticism. Feedback is best when it motivates the client along the continuum and enhances the performance of the engagement. Always lead a client in truth, giving both positive, and perhaps "negative" feedback. Then help the client act upon it. You are there to assist your client with a solution on how to move forward on whatever their problems might be. Be in integrity when you are leading your clients. You want to inspire them to be more productive, to reach their goals, and to be working more as part of their team. You also want to make sure that you are demonstrating the value that you find within the client or the client's organization. Your clients are seeking problem solving and a good leader will also point out what is going well and what is going right.

Being a good leader within client engagements means you are developing the clients. Developing the client includes their self-esteem and also developing their skill sets, what it is they do, and how they perform. Developing the client also includes taking your client through continued improvement with training and development initiatives. This helps the client set achievable goals, allowing you to lead the client to reach those goals, with specific feedback so that they meet the objectives of your consulting agreement.

BE AN INSPIRATION

The best approach to motivating teams has to do with positive communication and helping the client communicate on all levels team–to-team and member-to-member. A good leader, in terms of the client engagement, requires being able to manage the client's emotions, not just our own. Things that come up with the client may be difficult, whether a professional stumbling block or a personal issue that seeps into the workplace. Either way, it is your role to foster positive working relationships in good spirit.

Being an inspiration to your clients and their team will enable everyone to get on the same page. Therefore, you need to make sure that everyone understands the organizational vision, and the vision of the consulting project. Each encounter, interaction, and meeting ends with you being the inspirational leader. Inspiration is a large piece of what you are bringing to the table as a leadership skill with your client.

BUILD TRUST

Trust is a key factor in every interaction you have with your clients. As a consultant leading the client team, you want to make sure that your team can complete the work agreed upon. Sometimes this means you go above and beyond to provide your team and your client with the best assistance to accomplish the task at hand.

Everything you do with your clients needs to position you so that they see you as trustworthy. The more forthcoming and trustful you are perceived to be, the more that clients will openly share so you can be of greater benefit to them.

Building trust with employees, clients, teams and managers requires that you are clear about what information is confidential and what information may need to be shared with upper management. When you are sitting down with an individual employee or team where you expect them to reveal information that will go up to someone higher in the organization, the employees always need to know. Sometimes you will be working with an employee or team that is telling you some things in confidence that you can share with the organization, however, without using names. Always be upfront about what is confidential and what is open. This way people in the organization never feel that you violated their trust. If anyone believes you have done so, the chances of the engagement being successful will be slim.

CONDUCT PROGRESS REVIEWS

The progress review is a critical tool to managing the engagement and leading the client as well as leading the team. It is the periodic pause to make sure that you are sharing your findings and gaining buy-in from your client. The progress review serves multiple purposes.

First, this is communication to the senior client leadership who want to know if the project is on track or not. The senior management team wants to know where you are exactly and how things are progressing.

Second, the progress review is an organizing moment in time that is a forcing mechanism to make sure that everyone is completing tasks before certain milestone dates. It is effective for your consulting resources, for the client, and for the client's team members, so that people know what work needs to be completed before the progress review date.

Third, the progress review is a great reinforcing mechanism to synthesize all the different work that is being done into a comprehensive and cohesive story. This review helps to take the separate pieces of work, separate analysis, and separate implementations and then tie them all tying together towards the meaningful end result that your project seeks to achieve.

The purpose of the project reviews are to demonstrate throughout your entire engagement that you are indeed on track or are calling attention to any issues along the way as you go. At the end of your project, no surprises are allowed. Everything needs to be known and the client should be thrilled with your results largely because of how you manage their expectations and provide feedback about the engagement using the progress review along the way as you go. The progress review is a great way to get time on people's calendars when they are too busy to meet with you on a day-to-day basis. With that said, the best client engagement processes are those that have an infrastructure with regularly scheduled meetings that keep clients totally in the loop on a daily weekly and monthly basis.

We recommend doing a progress review every single month, and for short projects more frequently. You might want to reiterate the vision for the project. This way you make sure that everybody is still on the same page about the goal of the project. It is your way of double-checking that both you and the client still have the same vision, clarity, and understanding of the current reality. During the progress review, you can discuss what has been happening over the previous week or thirty days and establish exactly where you are in present time regarding the client's goals. You can then determine what you want to do next and what the plan is for the next month or so with the client.

When you sit down for a client review, you will review the action plan that supports the goals and vision of the client. During the review, you then illustrate your accountability to the client and assess the client's accountability as well. These progress reviews, along with accountability from both parties, are why client engagements are successful. Think of these review sessions as check-ins to talk about milestones and resources, as well as ensure that you and your client are on the same exact page at all times. The review sessions allow you to be certain that there is no error at the end of a contract with a client saying you did not do what you were supposed to do or "I didn't know this was going to happen." Again, we strongly suggest that you do a project review at least every single month with longer projects, and weekly with shorter ones. This will insure you and the client have full agreement and you are moving the project toward the agreed upon collaborative goals.

During a client progress review you can use the coaching skills of identifying the gap. Ascertain the gap between the vision of where the project is going and the reality of where the project is in this thirty-day (or weekly) period. Then you, along with the client, can determine what you need to do and then come up with a joint agreement and then get into agreement going forward.

INFLUENCE YOUR CLIENT TO TAKE ACTION

The last skill we will talk about among this critical list of advanced skills is influence. The reason why influencing is so important is that you, the consultant, are an outsider, and you, the consultant, do not own the results for that company. Your client must take total ownership of the consulting project and the results from the project. Your client needs to have accountability to their end result and understand that it is their actions and their decisions (even though they may be following your recommendations and strategies) that are key to achieving their results. It is up to your client to make things happen. Your job is to convince clients of the right path and to influence them to take the steps necessary to make your suggestions a reality to them.

One of the most frustrating parts of being a consultant is seeing with 20/20 vision and great clarity what a company needs to do and predicting with tremendous accuracy the benefit they will achieve as soon as they do whatever it is you're asking. But then, they do nothing, or they attempt, but give up, or they half-heartedly follow through on your recommendations only to allow their existing culture and work method to overshadow any changes and knock them back to where they were in the beginning. It will drive you crazy because you care so much about their success, and yet they won't do what's required to help themselves out. Sometimes you may even have laid out the step-by-step plan with such detail that all they have to do is follow the recipe.

This is where influencing comes into play. You are influencing human beings to change behaviors, make decisions, and take action. You are motivating clients to get excited about what is possible and to have the courage to make, what may feel to them, tough decisions. If you always act with the highest level of integrity for what is best for your clients, then you will help clients to see what is best for them. Only then can you feel your job can be complete.

Influencing means you are making sure that you have mutual communication around problems, situations, and solutions. You cannot effectively influence unless you and your client are on the same page and have some agreement. To be an influencer, and in order to bring solutions to an organization, there has to be a mutual conversation around those solutions. Even though you may be the consultant with the answers, the organization needs to feel as if they are involved in finding their solutions, by actively participating in the problem solving and the brainstorming. While your client is looking to you as the expert, the best way to influence is to include members of the client's team into the decision-making. This way they will own the ideas along with you. Whenever you are solving problems, mutual agreement on the action steps is essential for project success. Additionally, as an influencer, be certain you always follow up. Whenever there is an action to be taken by the organization and the team, ensure them that there will be some type of follow up and that you and/or your team will always check in that the actions have been taken.

A good influencer will also recognize achievements. People respond better when you are guiding them, praising them, and noticing what they are doing well and what they are doing right. The coaching skills we mentioned earlier, like powerful questions, can be very valuable to an influencer, as can the skills of powerful observations and powerful requests. These three separate coaching skills tie in extremely well to being an influencer within a client's engagement—assisting in brainstorming to create solutions to your clients' challenges. (See Chapter 13 for more information on these skills.)

ADVANCED SKILL WRAP-UP

To wrap up this section and our conversation about consulting skills, remember that from a place of personal development and continuous improvement, whatever skill level you have today is enough for you to start with your first client. Be open-minded and recognize that there is a lot more you can achieve and develop as you expand these skills further. The more effective you are at applying these skills, the more quickly you can have impact for your clients. The more impact you have for your clients, the more money you can make in consulting fees, either through your time, or your team's time. Develop the skills, create the impact, and grow your revenue.

**Remember, for bonus resources
related to this chapter, go to:**

www.TheUltimateGamePlanBook.com/resources

CHAPTER 13

• • • • • • •

MAXIMIZE YOUR IMPACT—BEFORE YOUR CLIENT ENGAGEMENT

THE MAXIMUM CLIENT IMPACT MODEL™

We have created the *Maximum Client Impact Model*™ as a way to describe how you can add value at every step of your engagement. The process actually begins with how you prepare and make decisions before you even have a signed engagement letter or contract for your client work.

There are two sections for this model and then elements within each section. Within this chapter, we describe the model and then go into detail behind each of the elements so that you can understand what you need to do to maximize impact for your clients. Here is the breakdown of the model for you:

Section 1: *Before* Your Client Engagement

* ✶ Element 1: *Develop* Frameworks to Align with Your Market Positioning
* ✶ Element 2: *Diagnose* and Assess the Current Situation
* ✶ Element 3: *Determine* the Right Problem to Solve

Section 2: *During* Your Client Engagement

* ✶ Element 1: *Draw* Your Client In and Engage Them In Your Process

* ✶ Element 2: *Disseminate* Information and Create Communication Channels

* ✶ Element 3: *Define* Metrics and Regularly Confirm Results

* ✶ Element 4: *Deploy* Strategies and Action Plans

* ✶ Element 5: *Discuss* Progress and Celebrate Success

In this chapter, we describe the elements of Section 1, Before Your Client Engagement. We describe the elements of Section 2, During Your Client Engagement, in the next chapter.

Before Your Client Engagement contains three elements: Develop, Diagnose, and Determine. Develop frameworks to align with your market positioning. Diagnose and assess the current situation. Determine the right problem to solve. We dive into the details behind each of those specific elements so that you can understand what they mean and exactly what it is that you need to do before you have an agreement in place for your consulting engagement.

ELEMENT 1: DEVELOP FRAMEWORKS TO ALIGN WITH YOUR MARKET POSITIONING

We touched on frameworks earlier in Chapter 8. Here we go into more depth about why building your proprietary frameworks is important beyond marketing. They will provide structure for your consulting engagements.

A framework is a basic conceptual structure that underlies a system concept or text. A framework is important for you to create for a couple reasons. First, it helps you to clarify your thinking in such a way that you can now create a cohesive image or pattern to help you pull it all together. Second, it helps you communicate your concepts to others.

In some cases, we have two-dimensional or even three-dimensional graphics that we have sketched out and then had our graphic artist create something that can be used in presentations, embedded into the book, or placed on the website. Other patterns include acronyms including SMART Goals where S-M-A-R-T is a framework in goal setting. Pete has a keynote called the "5 Cs of Goal Achievement" where the 5 Cs represents a framework. They are Cascade, Create, Commit, Confirm, and Celebrate. You might even notice in this chapter that each of the elements we're discussing start with the letter D. That itself is a framework.

The point about creating a framework is to help you to become clear about the concepts and principles that are running through your mind. Once you have your thinking clearly represented, it is so much easier for you to describe this to other people—your clients in particular.

Your frameworks are foundational for so many other things. Yes, of course, they describe your thinking and approaches in a client conversation. But beyond that, you can describe this framework in your marketing materials, put it up on your website, write blogs about your framework, build a keynote for speaking engagements, or even create training materials behind your framework. Or you can embed your framework into other speaking engagements and presentations. The "picture" of how you think will make it so much easier for someone else to come along with you.

So how do you create a framework? Imagine that you're sitting in a coffee shop with a friend having a conversation, and they're asking you questions like, "So how would you approach this?" Or, "Here's a situation...what would you do about that?" And then you grab the napkin and your pen, and you start saying the following words, "The way I like to think about it looks like this..." You sketch and talk at the same time, sometimes it's a picture, sometimes it's words, but at the end of that conversation, *voila!* You have your framework!

That framework might be rather specific with the conversation at hand, or it might be more broadly applicable to more general situations, and that's an important point in itself. If you were to sit in Starbucks with a line of people, one after another coming up to sit with you and asking the same type of question, "Here's my situation. What would you do about it? How would you approach it?" And you began each answer with, "Well, the way I think about it is..." You would end up with a stack of napkins all with nicely drawn frameworks and descriptions. Over time your frameworks would start to converge to a common understanding as your thoughts gel into something more cohesive and universal.

For example, as Pete was creating the Business Transformation Framework for his consulting company, he went through a number of iterations in order to create this framework. Not that he was sitting in Starbuck's holding court, but he was noodling, drawing, and sketching out a number of pictures and concepts on paper until he felt he had one right. The *Win Holistic Transformation Model*™ is the end result of this thought process that developed over a period of time. His framework represents how a company ought to think about its transformation journey all laid out in a full graphic. Interestingly, the framework has changed slightly over the years as elements within it slightly shifted and his perspectives progressed. Even though, the fundamental framework is the same. You might find that's true for your frameworks as well because you will evolve your thinking over time as you gain more experience and have more "ah-ha" moments.

Similarly, we created the *Power Up Formula* when we were preparing to deliver a webinar. We then went further and represented it as a circle graphic when we started conducting our live workshop, *Power Up Your Consulting Business.* It perfectly lays out the discussion about why you need to continue to deliver amazing value to clients. (To see the Power Up Formula represented in the circle graphic, look at the resources we provided at www. BusinessConsultantInstitute.com/ultimategameplanresources.)

The PACK Model is another framework that we described in this book. All of Section IV talks about the marketing steps Position, Attract, Convert, and Keep.

FRAMEWORKS LEAD TO OTHER FRAMEWORKS

What's interesting is that there could be other frameworks that you develop to describe the details behind elements within your primary framework. The same process holds true when you think about that specific topic. For example, within the *Win Holistic Transformation Model™*, Pete's business transformation framework, there's an element called *Conscious Leadership*. Conscious Leadership has its own three-dimensional framework to describe that leadership model and philosophy.

We're spending a lot of time discussing frameworks with you because it's so important for you to clarify your thinking and lay it out in a way that other people can quickly get what you're saying. We want your clients to quickly understand and resonate with your point of view. Once they understand who you are, how you think, agree that they line up with your thinking, and decide they need your help because of the way you approach problems and think about things, you can then turn the conversation into one that describes how exactly you can help them.

AN EXERCISE:

We want you to get rolling now and create some frameworks that represent who you are and how you think. Go back to your Core Unique Positioning Statement and look at the list of problems that you solve for clients. What's unique about you and your consulting company's approach? What is it that you do that's different from what other people in your space might do?

Imagine sitting in Starbuck's with your target client. They are asking you about the problems and challenges that they have and you are describing, with your pen and your napkin, what you are thinking is the best way to address their issue. What does that picture look like? Sketch out at least two or three different concepts of what your framework could look like.

ELEMENT 2: DIAGNOSE AND ASSESS THE CURRENT SITUATION

To diagnose is the exercise that a doctor would go through when you come in and say, "I've got this problem, doc." Before the doctor jumps to a solution, they need to ask you some basic questions, maybe go through some quick functional tests, and perhaps send you off for some other lab testing, etc. before they can pull all of this data together and make a decision about their diagnosis of your problem. Understand that there's a difference between doctors, just as, by the way, there are a variety of styles between consultants. Some doctors make a judgment based on their biases very quickly as they rush through their patient list, write prescriptions for their favorite pharmaceutical solution, and send you on your way. Others will spend a little bit more time probing deeper, asking more questions, and maybe discovering that the pharmaceutical solution isn't the right approach. For either doctor, there is a process they are following. One is following a rapid path to a quick solution that they hope will do the job quickly (and if that doesn't work they will try something else). The other is a little bit deeper to make sure that they're looking at other possibilities before they make their diagnosis and recommend the path of action.

As a consultant, the same process is true for you. You need to decide which type of doctor you're going to be. Are you going to be the consultant who makes a quick judgment based on a handful of tools that you like to use over and over with your clients and then suggest that's the answer for them? Or are you going to appreciate the nuances of every company and client's detailed situation before prescribing your strategies and your approach?

Pete was on a call recently with a contractor who was looking for Pete's company to help with the contractor's potential client that was much bigger than he could handle. (Remember, your contractors are free agents and often have their own consulting clients in addition to work they do for you.) The contractor's client is enormous with hundreds of locations across the US. This particular contractor had ascertained in a phone call that what they needed to do was implement 5S across all locations to solve a problem that tallied up to cost the client millions of dollars. 5S is a framework that originated in Japan with the Toyota Production System set of principles. (Note: 5S is a framework. There are 5 words all beginning with the letter S that drive cleanliness, orderliness, and discipline in the workplace.) Pete's team declined to work on this project because they saw it as applying a tool like prescribing a pharmaceutical solution which might make the client feel better that there was some action, but probably would not actually solve their multiple million dollar problem nor save them any significant money.

You might think of diagnosing like when your family mini-van develops some noise or rough running. You take the car into the mechanic and ask them, "Can you fix that noise?" Or, "My car seems to be running rough." And the mechanic fixes your car.

Some consultants are all about fixing things. If you have a diagnostic process to help identify what's wrong, what's broken, then you can become great at fixing things, provided you fix the right thing.

Other people are driving cars like those you might see on the racetrack or like those in the *Fast and the Furious* movies. They want to find a way to improve the performance of their car. They know all about efficiencies and ratios, and if they switch out this standard part for some enhanced part, the car should be able to go *ten* miles an hour faster. That's another type of consultant you can choose to be. You dig deeper to upgrade the performance of a business that's already performing well, but is not at its full potential.

THE DIAGNOSTIC PROCESS

In either case, you want to start with a diagnostic exercise so that you can appreciate the real problem that you will be solving and the real opportunity that your client has for improvement. This is taking the theoretical and the hypothetical and turning them into practical evidence so that you can understand what your client can achieve and accomplish in a relatively short period of time. That short period of time might be an outline for a two-year agenda or it might be something that itemizes the next six months of activities to get some quick hits. Both of those are important.

As you're conducting your diagnostic, you are also convincing yourself that you can actually help this client out. Once you're clear that you can help, you also need to describe the total opportunity. Paint a picture for them of what the future state could look like. Relate this to: their financials, their operating metrics such as how productive they can be, how much cost they can reduce, how it will be easier to deliver their product and services, the impact on customers, and the amount of revenue growth they can experience. Turn all of your ideas into real dollars, real meaning, and provide a prediction of what is possible for them based on the financials of their business.

Part of your diagnostic is likely to include an exercise where you dive into their financial statements and understand the basics of how their business is running today. From that baseline of understanding, you can then predict the impact that you will have with the initiatives to either solve the problems or to bring them up to the next level of performance improvement. Then translate this into a financial value for them. It's not unusual that your diagnostic exercises will itemize a total of millions of dollars of impact for your client.

ELEMENT 3: DETERMINE THE RIGHT PROBLEM TO SOLVE

Now that you've completed your diagnostic exercise and you have had the opportunity to:

* take your long list of potential problems and your hypotheses about the most important problem

* review your analysis and have narrowed your focus to a handful of problems that you think are the ones that you must solve first

* determine that the aspiration for your client is not one based on solving problems but delivering a higher level performance

You know the most important levers to pull to get that desired level of performance.

Determining the right problem to solve and the right levers to pull is critical for a few reasons. First, you want the fastest path to impact. If you pursue the wrong problem, you might spend a lot of energy on something that just doesn't deliver impact quickly enough to satisfy the client and your high level of aspirations as their consultant.

Second, you don't want your resources spinning their wheels on something that just doesn't matter. The client resources required to pursue different consulting engagement initiatives can be quite extensive and disruptive to their company's operations. You want to make sure that their team members are put to good use so that they feel that they are making a difference.

Additionally, if you have a large consulting team working on this client project you want to guarantee that your consulting team resources are effectively working on things that matter.

Third, you want results that are meaningful and create credibility for your strategies and advice as quickly as possible. Working on the right problem and seeing quick impact, where the resources feel like they are producing results that matter, will quickly build your relationship with your client and give you a higher level of credibility for future advice that you will continue to provide throughout your relationship with this client.

As you complete your diagnostic and you've developed your point of view about the right problem to solve and the right levers to pull for the client to achieve higher levels of performance, it's important for you to gain consensus with the client so that they agree with your point of view. You need to synthesize your diagnostic exercises down to the salient and coherent point or points that describe the "answer." Scope out the different initiatives that you would recommend that your client follow and then to gain buy-in or synthesize your perspectives or recommendations with critical client managers, executives, and team members. You're seeking consensus and also earning the right to continue supporting this client because of how you've interacted with them and how you've impressed them with your data collection analysis and conclusions as a result of your diagnostic exercise. You've now determined the right problem to solve and are gaining their buy-on to then motivate them to take action and to give you the permission to continue on guiding them as their consulting partner.

So you've developed your frameworks that helped clarify your thinking and shared your thought processes with your clients, you've launched a diagnostic exercise so that you can assess and understand the current situation, and you've determined the right problem to solve. If you've sufficiently impressed your client with the work you've done so far, you can now walk away with a signed contract, engagement letter, or task order that scopes the actual engagement that you're about to start. Congratulations! You now have a client project you are about to launch!

Remember, for bonus resources
related to this chapter, go to:

www.TheUltimateGamePlanBook.com/resources

CHAPTER 14

• • • • • • •

MAXIMIZE YOUR IMPACT—DURING YOUR CLIENT ENGAGEMENT

IN THE LAST CHAPTER WE described Section 1 of the Client Impact Model, *Before* Your Client Engagement. In this chapter we will describe Section 2, *During* Your Client Engagement.

During Your Client Engagement contains five elements: Draw, Disseminate, Define, Deploy, and Discuss. Draw the client in and engage them in your process. Disseminate information and create communication channels. Define the metrics and regularly confirm results. Deploy strategies and action plans. Discuss—review progress and celebrate success. These elements are crucial to ensure your engagement is successful.

ELEMENT 1: DRAW YOUR CLIENT IN AND ENGAGE THEM IN YOUR PROCESS

Draw your client into your process right at the beginning of your relationship and at the launch of a new project. Have a kick-off event, a meeting that allows your client sponsor to introduce the problem or the aspiration, describe why the client has chosen to launch this project, and that they have decided to partner with you, (and that's a key word, *"partner"* with you) as their consulting support to help them achieve the goals that they've set. This is the opportunity for them to get to know you. Your client sponsor will introduce you and your team from your consulting company as well as include key members of the client resources who have been selected to participate actively in this project. Ideally, you would have talked about some of this ahead of time and there will be a team leader and other client team members present. Announce these roles at this kick-off meeting so everyone knows the key players from both the client's and your consulting teams.

Depending on the size of this particular engagement, you might have multiple project teams that will launch all under an infrastructure with a master team leader from the client and a master team leader on your consulting team. There's a governance structure that we strongly recommend that involves people from your client team as well as people from your consulting team. Formal daily, weekly, and monthly touch points between the consultant and the client are highly recommended.

The daily communication can be an update meeting or simply a touch base where your consultant team leader meets with the client team leader just to confirm what activities are presently taking place right, what challenges have been raised, what barriers might be removed, and what the plans of action are for the next steps.

A weekly progress review might involve some other constituents from the client site. This is an opportunity for the client sponsor of this project to ask questions of the client team leader and the consulting team leader to make sure they are in the loop about progress and challenges that are uncovered. We don't want any surprises along the way during the engagement.

As for a monthly governance, we suggest a client steering team or executive team meeting where the client team leader and the consulting team resources have the opportunity to present progress, challenges, and plans to the executive in a summary way. If you have multiple project team leaders, this is an opportunity for them to have some face time with their executives. That is one of the biggest benefits of bringing a consulting team on board for a client. The client team members deeper in the organization probably do not normally have visibility or the opportunity to interact with executives. This is an occasion for them to show their stuff.

Drawing the client in and engaging them in your process is also a chance to share the day-to-day operating concepts that you want to lead with as you drive your client teams to take on the right activities with the new principles that you are injecting into their awareness. This will enable them to solve the problems and to raise their performance up to the next level.

As you describe the process, it is also critical that you clarify the roles and expectations of the different people that you are plugged into. Consider roles such as the team leader, a team facilitator, and the team members, plus consider your executive sponsors and the other executive team members and how you expect them to interact with the team. There's work that needs to be accomplished and completed, there's communication that's required, and there are results that need to be achieved and measured and then communicated. You will want the feedback on how you're doing, as well as communicate your progress so that other people who are constituents of this project can know what's going on.

Terri put these teams and team meetings in place in every client engagement and refers to them as *Transformation Teams*. In Pete's company, they are called *Breakthrough Teams*. Whatever you choose to call them, make sure you have this process defined.

ELEMENT 2: DISSEMINATE INFORMATION AND CREATE COMMUNICATION CHANNELS

The most successful client engagement exercises and projects include a very clear structure where you, as the consultant, can share progress with your client team. This is where the governance structure comes into play with the daily communication, the weekly progress reviews, and a less frequent, perhaps monthly progress review discussion. But having that structure laid out is only part of the issue. What you also need to do is gain buy-in from the clients at the executive and manager levels so that you understand how they want to receive communication from you and how they want to be involved in the project. Hopefully, the governance structure outlined will provide the majority of infrastructure for this to happen.

Some executives want to have one-on-one meetings with you more frequently. They prefer that you to give it to them straight in a closed-door, one-on-one conversation rather than wait for an open-forum team meeting. This is where you need to have the flexibility to build this into your structure. Additionally, there may be issues that you uncover that you do not want to air openly before first handling them in a one-on-one conversation.

You want to create the communication channels that enable you to have discussions like this when they are required by the client or by you.

It's also a good idea to ask explicitly: Who else needs to be plugged into your project? Who else needs to be informed about the results? Who needs to be consulted before we launch any major changes?

The RACI framework helps in consulting engagements as well. RACI stands for Responsible, Accountable, Consulted, or Informed. It's a useful matrix tool to figure out who the key constituents are, and with every major decision, know who's responsible, who's accountable for making it happen, who needs to be consulted before you take it on, and who needs to be informed about what it is you're doing.

You want to share the "what" and the "how" as you go through these exercises. Make sure that if people are struggling you can put mechanisms in place to catch them before they fall flat on their faces. This is true not just for client team members, but for your consulting resources as well. If you have a team of consultants on a project and each of your consulting team members have responsibility for different parts of your overall engagement, you want to know whether or not one of your team members are struggling, if they need help, and what you can do to keep them on track.

Let's face it, from the client's perspective every individual on the client team is yours and you need to make sure that your team succeeds because it is your company name and your brand that matters. We like to say, "When in doubt, simply ask."

Ask:

* How do you prefer that we communicate with you?
* How do you prefer we share information?
* If XYZ situation were to come up, how would you like us to handle that?

In each case, be as proactive as you possibly can.

ELEMENT 3: DEFINE METRICS AND REGULARLY CONFIRM RESULTS

While your processes to disseminate information and create communication channels are important, what also matters is having some agreed upon metrics that define your level of success. Agreeing to these ahead of time, perhaps even before the engagement launches and you have your formal kick-off, is critical to tracking results.

Ask yourself this question, "What does success look like?" Determine what success looks like from your client's perspective first and then from your perspective. You always want to remember your client's perspective and what's most important to them. Also, tie your success criteria back to the diagnostic that you presented to the client before this engagement was confirmed.

Note what you said were going to change as a result of launching these initiatives and projects. Think of it in terms of the operating metrics as well as the financial metrics.

* How much more productive?
* How much quicker can the work be completed?
* What will the customer experience be?

* What will the employee experience be?

* What is the quality level, delivery level, productivity level, and efficiency level?

* And then how much cost were you able to liberate?

* How much new revenue were you able to bring in?

* How much inventory were you able to release?

Fundamentally, the financial drivers are revenue, cost, and working capital.

You don't need metrics for everything and that might not be productive. However, it is critical that you track the most important elements that align with what you described as initiatives. Guide the client in defining what they will deliver as well as the targets. Determine how you will measure success. Be sure to track those and keep an eye on these for the executives and with the executives as you make progress implementing your strategies.

ELEMENT 4: DEPLOY STRATEGIES AND ACTION PLANS

It's one thing in a diagnostic or a client proposal to list out a number of strategies that you recommend in order to get the results so that your client will get moving from their current state of operations to some new better future state with higher levels of performance. It's another thing to take those strategies and make it clear what the action steps are.

* What are the action plans that you will lead them through?

* What does the Gantt chart look like to provide the overview of steps and timing?

* What are the steps?

* Who owns each step?

* Who are the other resources that need to be involved?

* What timing do things need to be completed by in order for you to be successful within the time frame that you promised you would have things completed?

With the clarity that you've defined those metrics, you can now ensure that the action steps that you are deploying will deliver the results according to the timelines expected. This translates into targets associated with each metric that you are expected to hit. The best action plans actually have a sense of impact that each of the action steps will deliver toward the metric that it is designed to deliver.

So for example, if you have a goal to increase revenue by $1 million, your action steps should all have some revenue amount that they're expected to deliver as a result of taking those action steps. If all of these steps add up to a million dollars or more, then you know you have an action plan that is adequate to deliver the results that you have defined and your executive sponsors expect. If the steps you have and the predictions you have for the impact of each step do not add up to the million dollars, then you know your action plan is still incomplete and you will require more specific things to do for you to hope to be successful.

Strategy and action plans have a few elements that are really important.

* Who is the owner of the strategy?

* How do you measure success of that strategy?

* What are the specific steps required to hit the targets defined by the metrics?

* When is the best time for those specific steps take place in order for you to be successful?

* Who is responsible for completing each step?

* What other team members do you need to have plugged in to help support implementing these steps?

* And then, of course, consider RACI that we described earlier. Who else needs to be consulted and informed along the way?

Unfortunately, too often we have seen an action plan that is extremely well written, but then there has been no exercise to gain buy-in from other people who have a say in how work gets done. It's not that other managers are trying to block your progress, but unfortunately that sometimes is the result when you do not engage them on the front end.

You're probably starting to understand clearly how all of these elements are important so that you can maximize impact with your client engagement. Draw your client in and engage them in your process. Disseminate information and communicate well. Define the metrics so you can measure success. Deploy your strategies and action plans. All of this leads us to the next element, which is Discuss progress and celebrate your success.

ELEMENT 5: DISCUSS PROGRESS AND CELEBRATE SUCCESS

Discussing progress is the element of formal communication, hopefully aligned with the governance model that we described earlier so that your client sponsors and executives can appreciate how you are doing towards the goals that you've set for this project. If you've managed to put in place all of the other elements that we've described here, then you will maximize your potential for success at your client. Your client team members can present at progress reviews and feel like heroes as they achieve results that are beyond their wildest expectations based on a sense of what is possible from their old paradigms. Now that you've introduced new principles and are expanding their definition of what is possible, that becomes very exciting. Then the real excitement kicks in when they have the opportunity to stand up in front of their boss, their boss's boss, their peers, and other team members to talk about the progress that they've made. This is a pivotal time for your client, and your role is to help them get pumped up and embrace the change that is possible for them. You inspire them to embrace the new reality that is *their* new level of results, and then ultimately, you encourage them to celebrate in the successes that they have achieved.

Helping your client to recognize the level of success that they are achieving is an important role for you to play as a consultant. You are teaching your client team members new business practices based on new business principles that you have introduced to them. When you continue to demonstrate that they are working, that will further emphasize for them two things: confidence in themselves and what is possible, and confidence in you and your advice as you continue to be their chosen advisor.

**Remember, for bonus resources
related to this chapter, go to:**

www.TheUltimateGamePlanBook.com/resources

SECTION VI

• • • • • • •

TYPICAL CLIENT PROBLEMS

Consultants are guaranteed to come face to face with a number of issues that their clients are dealing with—some which are obvious and on the table and others which appear after some probing. It's your job to discuss strategies to eradicate the issues—and you may also have to be the one to initiate a difficult conversation with your client about what you've discovered and what they may have tried to avoid tackling because the issue may seem overwhelming.

In this section, we'll discuss some of the problems that may be put on your plate as a consultant. While there are an infinite number of possible issues for which a client could ask for your support, we highlight the major ones in this section.

In Chapter 15, we talk about the common problems that create a drain on the company's financials. In Chapter 16, we discuss some typical organizational problems. As the consultant, you can recognize the problems and then walk them through solutions.

CHAPTER 15

• • • • • • •

KEEP THE GREEN FLOWING—SOLVING FINANCIAL PROBLEMS

JUST ABOUT EVERY CLIENT PROBLEM will have a measurable impact on the financials. Sometimes the problem is in one of the functional areas, like engineering or operations, and when you solve that problem your client will enjoy the financial benefit. Other times the financial performance is so poor (at least versus expectations) that you need to dive into the financial statements and figure out how to improve revenue, reduce costs, improve cash flow, etc. The solutions could cut across the entire business.

In this chapter, we describe various client problems, especially as they relate to the company's financial performance. Before we begin, let's get grounded on some financial basics.

BASIC FINANCIAL STATEMENTS

Here is a collection of some quick textbook concepts to make sure we are on the same page. Mark this page for future reference.

The most important financial statements you will review are the Income Statement, also called the Profit and Loss (or P&L),

and the Balance Sheet. You might also look at their Statement of Cash Flows or other detailed sheets that show portions of the above. Typically, you would look at the current year or rolling twelve-months, and have reference to past quarters or years to see how the company is trending. You might have the budget looking out the next twelve-months as well.

The Income Statement basically itemizes the Revenues, all the various costs, and then the "bottom line" or profit. There are also subtotals along the way, such as Gross Profit (revenue minus cost of goods sold), Operating Profit (Gross Profit minus costs of ongoing operations, including overhead and selling/administrative costs), and Net Profit (Operating Profit minus all other expenses). Other ways companies look at their bottom line and hold their managers accountable to a performance expectation include: Earnings Before Interest and Taxes (EBIT), and Earnings Before Interest, Taxes, Depreciation, and Amortization (EBITDA).

The Balance Sheet itemizes the value of all the company's assets, their liabilities, and the amount of equity in the business. Cash is one of the most important company assets, and you want to make sure there is enough cash flow to operate the business. Working Capital is another important measure, which is current assets minus current liabilities, and a measure of the company's ability to pay its short-term debt. Inventory is part of Working Capital and would need to be converted to the product when sold to turn into cash, so too much inventory is a poor use of cash.

COMPANY FINANCIAL PROBLEMS

When looking at a company's performance from the perspective of their financial statements, you can make some judgments about their performance and create a number of hypotheses about areas they should be able to improve. You might know something about the industry they are in and compare their financial statements to what you might expect. Look at certain ratios, like Inventory Turns, and draw some conclusions about their current performance. Review productivity improvement trends year over year, or investigate costs as a percent of revenue. If they are way off versus what is typical, you should be able to help them identify the root problems and make improvements.

Larger businesses will have advanced financial reporting with their in-house accounting staff that will enable them to pick apart the entire company operations to look for issues. A business is a rather complicated set of people, processes, and materials that come together to provide products or services for customers. Ideally, all activities are accounted for and can be reviewed. The larger companies, especially those publicly traded, have expectations they must meet. If they are not meeting their budget or the executive team's or owner's expectations, then they treat the situation like a crisis before it becomes a disaster.

You'll hear of high-level problems such as not meeting profit expectations, revenue shortfalls, or poor cash flow. You might also learn of problems at the next level such as lack of productivity, too much inventory, slow collections, etc. Each of these has financial language to describe the impact on the company due to how they operate the details of the business.

Smaller businesses won't have super detailed financial reporting. They probably have a P&L and Balance Sheet that their accountant or bookkeeper creates for them when they request it, but they often simply use the amount of money they have in their company's checking account as a measure of success. The smaller company problems could be the same as the larger business issues, but the way they think of these problems is much more simple—Cash Flow.

Cash flow is critical for every business, as it is like oxygen to the body. Without the ability to breathe cash into your operation, the company will shut down. Larger companies address issues, such as lack of productivity or decreasing revenue—or the opposite situation like growing revenues beyond their capacity to deliver—before they have threatening cash flow issues. Small companies that really only monitor their cash position might be caught unaware.

From a financial perspective, cash flow is a function of profit, converting other assets to cash (think of past investments in inventory that you now use), or financing you can get to inject cash into the business. If we stay away from financing in this discussion, because we're talking about your consulting to help improve your client's financial performance, you're left with a couple options: help them become more profitable, which is the result of more revenue and/or less costs, and to become more efficient with the assets they have, of which working capital is the place to start.

If you think of how a company gets into trouble, it is sometimes a specific event, but not always. Oftentimes it's the way the business is managed that leads to a strain on their financials. Company revenues could drop as a key customer cancels future orders. Expenses could rise in any area. These changes in revenues and costs each put a burden on profit, the main contributor to positive cash flow. Or, your client may have taken out loans in the past and now they have to make payments from the limited supply of cash they have on hand, which then restricts their ability to invest.

As the consultant, you will become somewhat of a sleuth to figure out what is causing the financial condition to deteriorate. Until you do, your improvement suggestions might not be on the root causes. Ultimately, you will work on specific elements of the company's operations to increase revenue, decrease costs, and improve working capital.

Let's talk about each of these.

INCREASE REVENUE

Fundamentally, revenue is the function of the price of what you offer and the volume that you sell. If you can sell more at the same price, your revenue will go up. If you could sell the same but at a higher price, your revenue will go up, too. If you could both sell more and raise your price, revenue goes up even more.

Help your client review opportunities to increase their sales volume by studying what their customers are buying, looking at adjacent markets, launching complementary products, entering new geographies, or even acquiring a new product or service. In each case, you want to find a way to deliver the higher volumes without raising your cost structure, at least as a percent of the revenue.

You could also help them increase revenue by conducting a pricing analysis to figure out what price the market would accept. Often you will find that companies have not raised their prices in a while, which creates an opportunity for the market to accept the increase.

There are times when the company's fixed assets are underutilized to the point that a price decrease to generate significant volume increases is the best answer. Andrew Carnegie did this with his steel company as part of his strategy to keep the mills at 100% capacity, which led to his becoming the richest man in the world.

DECREASE COSTS

Decreasing costs begins with you studying the financial statements and understanding the cost structure for the business in terms of both direct and indirect costs. This includes things like direct materials, direct labor, indirect labor, and all of the different overhead categories like executive salaries, rent, utilities, and so forth.

If you work with a lot of companies, it may be quite obvious that some of these costs are not in line with what you might expect for the type of business that your client is in. When this is the case, the challenge is to develop initiatives to help bring the costs back in line with what you would expect. Another exercise you, as a consultant, will want to do is to look at the cost buckets—that is each cost by type and see where the most cost resides. It's not uncommon for a manufacturing company to have greater than 50% of the cost structure be made up of direct materials. You might find that labor makes up 30%, leaving various overhead categories for the remaining 20% of the total cost.

There are a number of different types of consulting engagements that you might launch to address cost. For example, with direct material you might do a purchasing review to see if the prices of the different commodities are in line with what you might expect. You might help your client navigate finding the right suppliers and re-negotiating prices through a request for proposal (RFP) process. Within the labor category, the name of the game is productivity improvements. And there are number of initiatives that you could launch within the context of productivity improvements that could include implementing the full set of Lean manufacturing principles, which typically results in tremendous productivity gains by redesigning processes of how material and information flow through the company in a more streamlined and waste-free way.

Other overhead categories can be studied and improved upon to free up some cost as well. Be mindful of opportunities to make some changes that could create some cost-reduction. Some of these will be easier to identify and execute than others. Utilities are probably one of the more difficult issues to address because utilities cost is a function of equipment required to produce products or services, multiplied by the rates paid to the utility companies. With that said, when Pete was at McKinsey and Company, he led some diagnostic exercises at manufacturing companies where they researched utility costs as part of the effort to reduce conversion costs for these clients. The firm had an energy sector practice that maintained a database of utility rates by usage across different geographies. By knowing the client's usage rates, Pete and his team were able to tell the client if they were paying too much and provided them with information to renegotiate their rates to a lower tier.

One of the easier ones to tackle is freight cost. There are two ways that freight costs can be reduced right away: the first is negotiating with the freight suppliers to see if they will reduce rates. The second is to see what you can do about limiting the amount of freight that you need to ship—particularly with an erroneous sense of urgency. If the client is spending a lot on expedited freight, like next day delivery, this usually indicates that there is some problem, perhaps in production or sales. This underlying problem creates the costly freight issue, causing the client to spend extra money to get the material to the right place at the right time. Solving those problems, therefore, creates real cost savings.

Similar to the utility cost reduction example above, we know some consultants who are experts in freight costs and can decipher if clients are paying too high of a rate to the freight companies. It is common to see enormous reductions off published rates, but you need to know what is possible and have some expert information to guide your negotiation. You could be the consultant to develop freight reduction expertise, or you might know how to leverage one as an extension of your team when you need them.

If you happen to be an expert in the manufacturing principles and Lean transformation, then it's possible that you will find yourself capable of deeper levels of operational improvements. Even if you don't have the skill set, you can still use some of these principles and apply them to reduce some of the waste or non-value added work that you see in the systems.

Other initiatives that could lead to significant cost reduction include finding ways to reduce complexity in the business. One area of complexity tends to be in the number of SKUs (stock keeping units). Many companies find that they are holding inventory just in case the customer orders a part; however, the part often hasn't been made for years. You might convince your client that they would be better off killing that SKU, never producing it again, and selling off that inventory to reduce space required to hold it, as well as free up the inventory off of your balance sheet.

Problem-solving skills are important to have as a consultant and will definitely help your clients to reduce their costs. Remember, every problem that they have in their business likely turns into extra cost downstream in some way. If you can help them develop a problem-solving skill and methodology so they're capable of preventing problems in the first place or at least solving them quickly, you can also liberate millions of dollars of cost from your client's cost structure. You'll be seen as a hero and will be more likely to be called upon in the future for additional consulting work.

IMPROVING WORKING CAPITAL

Working capital is calculated as current assets minus current liabilities. Current assets are those that can be converted to cash within a year, such as accounts receivable (money owed to your client), inventory, and prepaid expenses (which enables your client to use cash for other purposes). Current liabilities are those bills your client should expect to pay within a year and include accounts payable (money your client owes for expenses) and short-term debt (the current portion of the loans).

Improving working capital could be as easy as collecting money that is owed to your client. If they do have a lot of receivables outstanding, making arrangements to receive the funds is one of the highest priorities. This can be accomplished by a simple phone call to the customers who have outstanding invoices to arrange payments sooner than later by offering a payment plan. You can help your client to do the necessary analyses to figure out where to find the easy money.

The biggest opportunity is often in reducing inventory as you can make operations more efficient. This is not always an immediate change, but some elements of inventory reduction can happen very quickly. Look to see if there is any inventory that has been sitting around for a long time. Maybe your client got a price break five years ago on a bulk purchase on some raw materials, but they won't likely ever use what's left. Or maybe they produced some products expecting a big run on orders, but they manufactured more than they sold. Go sell off that inventory! Help them with an inventory analysis to guide them on what to sell.

For longer-term inventory reduction, your client will likely need some pretty deep changes in their operations. This could be in your client's forecasting, capacity planning, purchasing, scheduling, production, and distribution processes. If you can guide them to approach these processes holistically from a Lean or Toyota Production System perspective, the inventory reduction could be enormous—perhaps more than 80%. The important thing to realize is this is not a Band-Aid, but a rather in-depth set of initiatives that cut across much of the operations.

IMPROVE BUSINESS PROCESSES WITHIN FUNCTIONS

The functional areas within a company might have some unique challenges or problems that must be solved to perform at their expected levels. For example, does new product development take too long? Does the order-processing department lose orders which causes extra phone calls to the customer service team? Are there quality issues with the product? Does the month-end exercise for accounting take too long to close the books? Are there supplier challenges that prevent the company from having material to produce? We can go on and on.

In addition to considering the problems that cut across departments, look within the functional areas, too. Think of product development, quality, customer service, operations, sales, or marketing—and every other functional area within the company. As the consultant, the point is to be able to recognize these challenges are in each of the functional areas. If you have deep expertise in the functional area, then you would have instinctive insights to help your client identify and solve those challenges.

For example, let's say that with product development, the amount of time to release a new product is excessive versus what customers expect and also is larger than what your competitors or your client's competitors are actually doing. This suggests that launching a project or initiative to help the client to reduce their new product development time would be a highly valuable exercise for them. You might lead an engineering analysis where you study their process and figure out how to crash the critical path to cut their overall lead time to a fraction of what it is and enable new products to be produced very quickly. When fully implemented, this new capability would turn into increased revenue and perhaps an improved margin by getting these new products out more quickly.

Think about this: there's a specific quality problem in the production process that absolutely needs to get fixed because this poor quality to the market is causing big headaches for your client's customers. You would lead the operation teams in problem solving and engage the engineering expertise to figure out how to solve this quality problem.

We can go on and on with every functional area and come up with more examples, but you get the idea.

As a consultant, you would also have some perspective to guide improvements with your client. For example, we believe that the productivity of any team or process can be improved by at least 10%, without expensive automation. Imagine if you could get 10% more done every day. Now, multiply that impact across the entire population at your client—you could be talking about millions of dollars in a larger organization! You can assist your client in studying their processes and design the initiatives to capture the savings.

Every problem, when solved, will have a financial impact. For example, fixing a quality problem will result in reduced inventory and labor as you eliminate the need for rework. Freight cost is reduced as you no longer ship product back or expedite replacement parts.

It's important to itemize the cost savings for every change you implement. You might be surprised to see how enormous your collective impact adds up to as value you deliver. Track and communicate this amount as part of getting the client excited about your contributions as their consultant.

**Remember, for bonus resources
related to this chapter, go to:**

www.TheUltimateGamePlanBook.com/resources

CHAPTER 16

. . . .

ORGANIZATIONAL CHALLENGES

IN LOOKING AT ORGANIZATIONAL CHALLENGES, it's important to take some kind of a diagnostic where you can assess the performance stats in each area of the company's organization to discern where the gaps exist. By identifying the baseline, the groundwork can be developed for a plan that you can refer to during your engagement. This way you'll be able to document where the improvements are, assuring the client that progress is indeed being made.

Conducting a diagnostic enables you to plot out how you want changes to happen, and how the organization wants changes to happen. Gaps can be discovered in the client's sales process, for example, and you can identify how to move projects forward so that there is more satisfaction with performance in each area of the organization. It's important to understand overall performance of an organization, acknowledging their challenges and pinpointing what changes would be ideal. Consider the organization as a whole—the team, individuals, and customers. Determine how effective the people are within the organization to produce the results that the company desires.

* Do they have the right skills, energy, and motivation?
* Are they working cohesively?
* Do they have a problem-solving attitude?
* Are people able to take ownership of their role?
* Do they own their own performance?
* Are people in charge responding to the need of the others?
* Do they need to be told what to do?

We also recommend looking at what is possible:

* What is it that the organization wants to achieve in the future?
* Are they talking as an organization about what is possible?
* Are they open to suggestions for improvements?
* Does the organization encourage and reward team member efforts?

As you look at the big picture of the organization—the organizational goals—ascertain if the individuals on the team know what those are, and if they understand how their role and their job actually connects to the overall organization's goals. It's really important that each of the members of the team see the bigger picture and appreciate that their individual performance affects the company's performance.

Before you even begin to address the challenges, establish how you and your client are going to validate the results that were effective in initiatives. Determine how to measure the changes such as the financial return on investment to know if a project is actually worthwhile and making a difference for the organization.

Here is a way to think about all of these organizational challenges: When you're not getting the results that you want, you have to remember that your processes have a technical set of steps that need to be followed to get results, but then within the company those technical steps are supported by people. There are so many dynamics with people and with how they function as individuals or as teams that your technical prophecies could be exactly perfect and yet your results are way below potential. When that is the case, investigate different areas within the organization for issues that might have a greater impact on cash flow than at first glance would be suspect.

Additionally, we have a sub list of possible problem areas for you to recognize: culture, leadership alignment, organizational structure, roles and responsibilities, poor accountability, talent and performance, and morale.

CULTURE

Culture is the sum of all of the employees' beliefs, thoughts, and behaviors. What's challenging here of course is the only thing that's visible are the behaviors—the actions that people take or things that they do and say. It's the invisible that wreaks havoc on an organization—the individual thoughts and the core beliefs they possess that are driving the way that they think and the way that they act.

If the culture is not supporting the organization, then it is definitely getting in the way. So if you observe the different behaviors and recognize those that are aligning with the direction that the company wants to go versus those that are impeding progress that gives you a clue to the culture's performance level. If it's not what is desired, then there are number of different initiatives that you would need to launch to shift the company's culture.

The way to know what initiatives are most appropriate is to conduct a diagnostic to uncover your client's specific culture issues. With that in mind, common initiatives that are important in most every company include launching teams to improve communication, to hear what employees think is important, and to create fun methods of engagement. With the millennial employee population growing, your clients will want to keep them interested or else those employees will likely move onto other companies. Leadership intervention with employees to create the culture your client wants is critical in shaping culture, so you can expect to help design specific leadership programs to create consistency in how managers and supervisors emphasize and reinforce the attributes of the culture they are creating.

LEADERSHIP ALIGNMENT

The second possible problem area is leadership alignment. One of the key elements for you is making sure that the critical functions of the leader makes sense to the organization and that the leadership is truly aligned with whatever the associated tasks might be. One of the other pieces is making sure that the leadership is positioned with the overall vision or goals of the company, and subsequently have the way to communicate, get the kind of recognition that is needed, and the planning tools in place. Then collectively, they can work through the barriers that are in the way as you guide them through the process of removing the barriers keeping them from achieving their specific goals. It's important to understand the function of each team, if the right people are on the team, and to document the barriers, so that they can actually be worked through.

One of the things that we do to align teams is to begin with identification and presentation of a complete list of barriers. You can do this by using coaching sessions where you really take a look at all the things that get in the way. It could be lack of: goals, leadership qualities, teamwork, discipline, information, or communication. Then you clarify and consolidate what you're hearing with the leaders.

Determine what's missing and identify if the leaders need training or team building. It could be a business process that would help them be more effective and remove barriers. Once you've identified the barriers, devise a leadership plan that may even involve some direct coaching of the leaders to get them better aligned personally as well as professionally.

So now the questions is: leadership alignment to what?

PURPOSE, VISION, MISSION, AND GOALS

Alignment is about aligning with the business, and aligning with the other leadership team members. Your leadership team most importantly needs to align with the company's stated purpose, vision, mission, and goals. Make sure that their behavior and energy is driving in the same direction that the company wants to drive. The second leadership alignment is to each other. Confirm that all of the areas of the company are heading in the same correct direction and that there are not any initiatives that individual leaders are driving, which are in conflict with what other areas of the organization are driving. When this happens, it's like paddling the boat against the current to try to get to your destination. When you can get everyone aligned, it's like paddling the boat with the current to get to your destination. You arrive much more quickly and effortlessly.

ORGANIZATIONAL STRUCTURE

This is sometimes a barrier that prevents the company from being effective largely because you might have people in the wrong roles. The ideal is to have the right people in the right roles in an organizational structure that is clear about areas of responsibility and how things get done. The diagnostic that you would do related to organizational structure is looking at decisions, how decisions are made in the reporting structures to know where people are getting their direction from, and how quickly they can move in order to respond to problems or complete projects. If this process is bogged down, and you notice that there are multiple layers of approval or too many people getting involved in decisions, then the organizational structure itself is worth further analysis.

ROLES AND RESPONSIBILITIES

This fits in very closely to organizational structure. Each individual on the team needs to have clarity about his or her role in the organization. They must understand their responsibilities: what they're accountable for in terms of results and what decision rights they have. It's vital for them to know when and where they need to get other people involved with decisions, with implementation, and simply with solving problems and making things work.

ACCOUNTABILITY: POOR OR LACK OF

One of the areas that is a major organizational challenge is a lot of times the goals of a team or an organization aren't even laid out in terms of SMART goals that are specific, measurable, and achievable to a related time scale. There are a multitude of different ways people language SMART goals. One of the things that is absolutely a golden rule of every organization is to make sure that people know what the goal bar is and that there is a way to measure that the goals are being achieved.

There must be accountability for goals, some type of a checklist or a monitoring system. It could be a daily meeting or a daily huddle. A tracking system for team performance indicators could be put in place. As a consultant, you may establish the way that the organizations will stay on track with their own internal measurables, as well as how you, as a consultant, will develop external measurables to make sure that team members, leaders, and individuals are accountable for whatever performance or task that needs to be done. This is really how you have an organization achieve their goals. There needs to be some blend of direction and support, while at the same time, some internal system of accountability where people are monitoring themselves.

In an organization with effective organizational leadership and accountability, there's an understanding of the task, the processes, the priorities, and the motivation. Additionally, the leader has a relationship with and understands the team members' preferred styles of communication so that they can agree to the leader's expectations. We also have to manage the specifics of whether or not goals are being reached. We can't manage that only on a monthly basis because by the end of a month we have wasted a lot of time. So setting up some way to continuously monitor results on a daily or weekly basis is optimal. This creates a real win-win situation organizationally and even for the individuals within an organization. Everyone knows what's expected of them, everyone knows how things get measured, everyone becomes accountable to themselves and to the organization, and everyone is working toward moving forward in terms of whatever the gaps may be.

Accountability comes from people understanding what they need to achieve and getting some form of both positive and constructive feedback so that they understand their value. Even if they may be off track with the goal, with some direction they can get back on track. With accountability in place, an organization isn't wasting any time or money, and *is* moving forward quickly because there is no waiting one, two, or three weeks to see whether or not people are achieving what they need.

A word of caution: During the diagnostic exercises you may hear phrases like, "I can't trust anyone to get things done." That's a trigger that there's likely an accountability issue in the company. Accountability means that people can be counted on to do what they say they're going to do, or to do what they're expected to do. It's a function of knowing what's expected and then a function of trust that they have the skill sets and motivation to do what needs to get done. If you identify that there is an accountability issue in the company, be aware that the business leaders might not yet be aware of how critical accountability is for the consulting project and for their long-term success.

TALENT AND PERFORMANCE

There is a large problem with many performance management systems in that they lack any real management capability. Managers in an organization very often can hide behind the system. This is largely due to the fact that performance can be subjective. To improve performance management, take a look at what's expected in an organization. Ensure that job descriptions are clear so that we know we have the right talent. Determine if management is performing objective appraisals by observing individuals' functional competencies and their behavioral competencies.

As the company's consultant, you might identify the function of each individual in relation to the company and any list out areas where they may not have the right performance. Bring in some coaching skills to improve that talent. One of the most impactful actions we can take is doing a 360-degree appraisal. This will find the answers to the major questions in terms of performance management:

* Does the company have the best culture?
* Are job descriptions clear?
* Does the company know who needs to fill each role?
* Have the roles been clarified in terms of skills, knowledge, responsibilities and even the different behaviors and results expected?

Very often it's hard to understand whether we have good performance. The company mindset must be that they're not going to spend all of their resources developing and implementing talent system if we can't retain the right people in the first place. Consider what will keep employees happy enough to stay for the long-term.

It's much better if we can understand what the roles are, identify the people we need to fill those roles, and then be very clear when they are at full performance. When they are at full performance, it's important to know how to get them to exceptional performance. And if we identify an area where someone is not at full performance if they're the right person on the bus, how are we going to then get them in a role where they can be productive and add value?

Performance reviews usually will enhance staff motivation and develop performance. These tools review the current performance as well as determine if the employee is the right person for the job. If the right talent is in place, question how that person can be encouraged to grow within the organization so that they stay for the long-term. At times, we inspire and motivate through coaching. Other times, group training may be ideal for continued development of talent.

ORGANIZATIONAL TALENT REVIEWS

This is an exercise that needs to be conducted periodically simply because of the technology changes and the dynamic needs of the business which change from year to year. For example, in the days before the Internet and websites, you did not need someone on your team who had the capabilities of a web designer or Internet technology person. Yet fast forward to today, and these skills probably do have a very important role in your business. As technology evolves, the individuals in those roles must continually be supported in the acquisition of additional skills to keep the company on a competitive advantage. When observing the client's talent, question what the company needs to do to be competitive, staying ahead of customer demands. Notice whether or not those required skill sets can be trained and developed in the existing team or whether or not searching the market place for someone who has those skill sets is required.

Recently, a client had outgrown the capabilities and skill sets of the existing Vice President of Finance. That person was really good at managing some of the small company tasks and skills, but didn't possess the right skills to bring the business to the next level as a larger company. That is a talent gap. In this type of scenario, it's important to then recognize that there are multiple options, and you must guide the client to determine whether to replace that existing person or have them report to a new boss who does have the right skill sets. It might be the person has all of the correct competencies and simply needs some more mentorship and education. They might be willing to go through training classes and get that experience. Or perhaps, the client should really part ways with that person and find a replacement. In this particular example, keeping that resource in role for the long term would only hurt that company's potential for growth and profitability given that their processes were becoming more complex as they became a bigger company.

MORALE

Higher productivity and profitability is directly linked to employee morale. Employees need to have motivation to stay within an organization. They must feel appreciated and they want to develop in their roles. While many people think that morale has to do with income and financial motivators, studies have shown that it really doesn't have to do that how much employee is paid. It has to do with how employees feel within an organization.

There have been various studies where employees rated what motivates them. Feeling appreciated, respect, and peer and boss recognition are all at the top of the list. Sure, money is on the list, but is below some of these other motivations that have to do with how they feel. We read a recent article in *Forbes* that described a survey that asked "What motivates you to excel and go the extra mile at your organization?" The article points out the same conclusion countless other surveys have identified about money: "Interestingly, money—often simply assumed to be the major motivator—was seventh on the list, well back in the pack."

During some training that Pete attended early in his career for managers about how to motivate employees, they discussed seven different "levels" that people go through during their lives, and what the primary motivators are at each level. Again, money is a primary motivator for only one of those seven.

What's been true for a long time is even more true now with more Millennials in the workforce. Employees have to be able to enjoy their job. They want respect and to be recognized for their achievements. And they also want to have feedback about their performance. If they're not feeling valued and acknowledged, chances are they will leave.

It's really important for an organization to have high morale. Employee morale comes from how committed they feel as the part of the organization, how motivated they are to do their particular job, and how confident they are, first in themselves, then in their direct manager, in the company and the company's future, and even in the products or services that the organization is providing. So as you look within an organization, you want to assess how people are feeling not just about what they're doing, but about how they fit in, about how well they are incorporated into a company or an organization.

The objective is best set that we're not only noting the employee's direct observable contribution in a form of workload. We really have to question how that person can be developed, and how we can help to create greater achievements for them so that they really feel that they are respected and appreciated within a company.

Engaged workers call out sick less, and have fewer injuries and workers compensation claims. They are much more committed to staying with the company long term, even if a better offer comes along. One of the most expensive situations for an organization is recruiting talent and training talent. A big part of employee morale is maintaining employees not just with their technical competencies, but also making sure that they have the right behavioral competencies and that we keep employees on board with the right attitude. They will be much more likely to stay with the company long-term—even if a better offer comes along.

When changes are poorly managed, morale can be negatively impacted. Imagine that the president of your company changed to a new business and a new guy was recruited in. Let's just say his style was a bit different from what people were used to and didn't really align with the culture. Rather than try to learn the cultural dynamics and how to get things done within the existing environment, he instead came in with an aggressive agenda and didn't bother to appreciate the team's efforts and accomplishments. You can expect morale issues across your client's entire organization to deal with. People might quit, even with your best efforts at trying to cheer them up and keep a positive perspective. The management team will be recruiting nearly full-time to replace the people who had left. It would be tremendously disruptive. It's your job as the consultant to intervene, and educate and coach the new president to prevent this from happening.

When you're looking at organizational challenges and recognizing that this is all about people, it's important you, as the consultant, appreciate that all of the different people in an organization have their own unique skill sets and perspectives, as well as their own unique styles. As a consultant or consulting team, you might consider having access to some of the different assessment tools that are available out there. Some of the popular ones are the Myers Briggs Type Indicator (MBTI) and the Human Brain Dominance Indicator (HBDI). These tools can give the employees a greater sense of self-awareness, as well as provide teams with an appreciation for the strengths and differences that their team members have. By raising this awareness across a team, you can actually improve teamwork and cohesiveness—and ultimately the ability to get things done.

**Remember, for bonus resources
related to this chapter, go to:**

www.TheUltimateGamePlanBook.com/resources

SECTION VII

* * * * * * *

OTHER IMPORTANT QUESTIONS ANSWERED

In this section, we have highlighted some of the biggest questions we receive from consultants like you that have not yet been covered in the prior sections of this book. Our mastermind clients and those who attend our *Power Up Your Consulting Business* events also ask the same kinds of questions so we thought it would be helpful to address them here.

In Chapter 17, we describe the differences between business consulting and business coaching. This is an important question because there are many business coaches who are under serving their clients and could gain some benefit by adding consulting skills. Also, the best consultants have coaching skills as part of their repertoire. Review this chapter to understand the differences and how they can be complementary.

In Chapter 18, we discuss the different members of your team. Even if you see yourself as a one-person consulting company, you really do need to have extended team members to make your company work smoothly and have access to expert advice. Read this chapter and make sure you have these critical team members in place.

In Chapter 19, we review the different legal business structures that are choices for you. Even if you already have a consulting company, you may discover from this chapter that the business structure you have selected for your consulting company is one that leaves you exposed. This chapter will get you smart enough to ask your attorney and CPA some important questions.

CHAPTER 17

• • • • • • •

HOW DOES BUSINESS COACHING RELATE TO BUSINESS CONSULTING?

Accoding to the International Coach Federation (ICF), there about 35,000 people calling themselves coaches. There is no exact accreditation for business coaches although some people choose to be members of the International Coach Federation. There is nothing that precludes somebody from just hanging a shingle and calling themselves a business coach, and there are all types of people calling themselves a business coach whether or not they have a degree in coaching. With consulting, it is more common for business consultants to have a background or direct experience in business. Recently, business coaching has become a degreed program with some colleges and universities offering degrees in coaching from a master's to a doctorate. There has been massive growth in both business coaching and consulting.

While the ICF has guidelines for coaching, we encourage you not to get hung up by strictly following the ICF definition. Rather, we suggest you call yourself a business consultant who has coaching skills. Potential consulting prospects understand what a business consultant does and also know that typically business coaches are paid a great deal less. We strongly recommend you be a business consultant who also uses coaching tools to help clients solve problems and grow your businesses. It is all about getting clients the outcomes they seek. We find you get better outcomes for clients when you utilize both coaching and consulting techniques when working with clients.

In our experience, doing business consulting for decades and mentoring our mastermind clients, we find it to be necessary to be a business consultant with coaching skills as clients need both. Clients hire us for business consulting and during our engagement with them, they ask us for practical advice, and want us to be a part of their brainstorming. When clients are seeking solutions and are mapping out strategies, they often stumble and need personal development work to lead to their success and that is where business coaching comes into play.

Coaching is helping a client discover their own answers and not necessarily giving the client your expertise. Instead of providing the answers, when you use your business coaching skills, bring in tools and resources like powerful questions, powerful observations, powerful requests to help the client look inside to discover their own answers. When in coach mode, you do not guide the client to the expertise that you, the business consultant, may have. And there is a time and place for both approaches.

As a business consultant who is also an expert coach, you can listen to your client's problems and hear how you need to best interact with them to solve their problems. In some cases, the client's problem will require your expertise as a business consultant to guide them and clients will want your help defining the strategies that will help them to achieve their goals. They may also want you to assist them with stretching their team skills and capabilities, challenging them to achieve more, etc.

In other situations, you may be hired as a business consultant to facilitate process improvement projects using your business expertise. Subsequently, you may be asked to design strategies, set up processes, and share your business tools, skills, and knowledge. Sometimes, you may be hired to actually do implementation of various systems and processes. While being called upon for your business consulting services, often you will also need to use your business coaching skills to help facilitate conversations or discussions. Business coaching skills are used in situations when you need to get team members on board with a particular initiative, and when you are creating strategy, designing corporate culture, and determining mission, vision, values, and determining which sandboxes the company could be playing in. Whenever you want to generate conversations and facilitate those conversations and have a client discover their own answers, you will use your business coaching skills instead of telling your clients the answers as their business consultant.

The most successful business consultants know when to use coaching skills in addition to their consulting skills. We have found that elite business consultants are able to switch back and forth between their consulting hats and their coaching hats. Clients typically hire a business consultant because they need answers and don't realize that sometimes guidance to find their own answers is actually the best approach.

Oftentimes in a workshop environment, a consultant is facilitating their clients to discover solutions to their key questions. In such a situation, you may notice that the client is heading down a wrong path or is coming up with some solutions that frankly will not be easy to implement. At this point, you need to be very directive and share the feedback with the company. The consultant's role becomes making it clear to the client that the path they are on will lead them to trouble. However, instead of giving the client a solution, you will begin using questions to guide the client to find their own answers to get back on track.

Sometimes you may see that the client does not really have any frame of reference other than their own business environment. This is when you, the expert, guides your client with specific strategies and gives them rather specific advice. When engaged in consulting, you might notice that a client is attempting to take on too much activity that they simply will not have the capacity to complete within a reasonable period of time. You might observe that the client is naive to some of the roadblocks that are right around the corner and maybe you have already run into these roadblocks before. Here, you can warn the company about the path they are on.

Our advice is to begin some of your business consulting contracts by building business coaching into the agreements. It's rare that a business coaching agreement becomes a consulting arrangement. It is almost always that the company hires you as their business consultant for certain expertise. They may require a change in operations, assistance facilitating a process, or establishing a strategy. The business coaching is an offshoot of business consulting. Companies hire business consultants for the "how to," and once they engage with the "how to" the business consultant may notice they need to use their business coaching skills to help the company or organization in the self-discovery process and in implementing their suggestions.

The coaching industry has been expanding over the past twenty years and a lot of companies have engaged business coaches during this time. Business coaching, when used separately without training facilitation or consulting, does not make significant changes within an organization. However, statistics show that when coaching is used in conjunction with facilitation, training, or consulting, long-lasting changes in an organization occur. Both *The Harvard Business Review* and a Sherpa Executive Coaching Study have documented these exact results.

As a business consultant, you will be able to serve your clients even better if you have business coaching skills in your tool kit as well. Business coaching allows you to help your clients create success by focusing on areas like personal development: time management, removing blocks, and self-sabotaging behaviors like procrastination, finding clarity, decision making, and goal achievement.

According to Diane Couto and Carol Kauffman, who wrote an article in *The Harvard Business Review*, entitled "What Can Coaches Do for You?" business coaches are "usually called executive coaches....Ten years ago, most companies engaged a coach to help fix toxic behavior at the top. Today, most coaching is about developing the capabilities of high-potential performers." So, it might be a good idea to polish your coaching skills right along with your consulting skill set.

Remember, the distinction between business coaching and business consulting is that when you are using business coaching tools you do not give advice. A business coach helps their clients discover the answers from within themselves. And a consultant shares their expertise. A highly successful consultant does both.

**Remember, for bonus resources
related to this chapter, go to:**

www.TheUltimateGamePlanBook.com/resources

CHAPTER 18

• • • • • • •

HOW DO I BUILD MY TEAM?

L ET'S TALK ABOUT FORMING YOUR team of support people for your business. We mentioned your professional advisors such as your attorney, your CPA, and your insurance agent. You may have a business coach or mentor that you want to enlist and give you guidance along the way.

Keep in mind the never-ending list of administrative tasks that have to be completed. You might add internal team members or outsource these tasks to people like your bookkeeper or a virtual assistant. In terms of doing the core consulting work, the burden will be on your shoulders until you expand and have enough work for more than one person. Only when you have more than you can handle should you consider pulling in other consulting resources either as employees or as contractor resources. We certainly find that building a team of employees slowly, while having a team of contractors available to access when you need them, is a sound strategy. (Remember Pete's story from Chapter 3? The last thing you want to do is have to have that difficult conversation with an employee stating that you can't meet payroll.) This way you can grow smartly while keeping your fixed cost base smaller rather than allowing your fixed cost to grow out of control with extra employees and payroll cost.

We suggest you conduct a regular review of your upcoming consulting workload and then decide how many more consultants you will need in your business. You might consider building relationships with possible contractors well before you need them. You will be responsible for the quality of their work, so be sure those consultants are qualified to do what your clients need from your team. Risking losing a client who could mean tens of thousands of dollars (or more) of contracts because you didn't do your due diligence is a bitter pill to swallow.

Here's the trick: Ultimately, do everything you can to keep your overhead expenses low and your flexibility high. While you build your cash flow, you might personally take on more work to keep costs down, but move responsibilities off your plate to others if you are constrained and not able to spend your time building your business with more clients.

This can be a tug-of-war on your time between you diving into client projects while trying to conduct marketing activities, network, and find your next client engagement. Cash flow is the real measure to indicate if you or your employees (already fixed costs) need to be the one for client work or if you pull in a new team member.

For example, in Pete's company when cash flow was tight, he asked the president of his consulting business (a fixed cost as an employee on payroll) to jump in to deliver some client work rather than assign it to a contractor, who is a variable cost. Pete often jumps in himself to lead shorter engagements like diagnostics, which has benefits in addition to assisting his company's cash flow because he gets to know the client and the consulting resources. This is not a great plan for the long term, but is a smart business decision in the short term to keep cash flowing.

Just remember, however, that there are benefits to having someone work with you in your business who can do the things that are not billable to a client, like opening up the mail, answering voicemails, invoicing, posting to social media, etc. that can ultimately save you time and money. Plus, it can be lonely sometimes to do everything yourself, so having another capable person around the office, even to offer another perspective, can be very worthwhile.

At a minimum, we recommend you have your accounting and bookkeeping handled—and an administrative assistant on board. Be certain you also have a team member who is knowledgeable about contracts. You must have contracts in place on all client engagements and also with employees or independent contractors. Contracts will protect you and make very clear who is doing what either inside your company or with your clients.

LEGAL DOCUMENTS

A contract is a legal document that involves two or more parties. In attorney language, there is an exchange of value—in other words, someone values your consulting services and provides you money in exchange for the value you bring to their organization or company. No matter how large or small the engagement is, make sure you have a contract so that you are protected. Your livelihood is truly at stake if something happens to go wrong so you need to have some type of documentation for all your business agreements as well as team member agreements.

A contract not only protects you, it also protects your clients and team members.

Contracts serve to make certain there are no misunderstandings and that everybody understands, in plain language, what it is that is being agreed upon and how payment works. Not only do you spell out your role as an employer to your team and your relationship to your contractors (that they are *not* employees), you also define your role as the business consultant to your clients. The team members and the client roles are also included in the terms of the agreements. This way everyone knows what is going to happen in the agreement.

Here are some common elements that a contract could include: definitions of terms and phrases; performances of services by contractor; term; relationship of parties; restrictive covenants; project scope; confidentiality; non-disclosure; non-solicitation; proprietary interests; indemnity; remedies. Talk to your attorney about what you require in your contracts. While this information is not legal advice, we hope you learn enough about contracts here to ask your attorney great questions.

Agreements must cover details like how and when you pay team members and how and when you receive compensation and reimbursement for the services you provide. Getting paid is the lifeblood of your business.

We recommend that you have an attorney create, or at least review your contracts, and all terms of your agreements. Ask your attorney to write your contact in plain English so your clients can understand the legal language, and request that contracts be kept short and simple. The shorter the better in our opinion as long as all key points are covered. The elements in most contracts include: fees to be paid, services being delivered, project objective goals, when the project ends, etc.

Contracts will also help you to avoid project scope creep. This happens when you begin a contract with a client and the client project has way more work than you agreed to do. Having a legal contract drawn up by an attorney will protect you because your contract will have spelled out exactly what you and the client specified in your discussions.

To avoid project scope creep, it is wise to also include the detailed description of the project with each very specific task that you have been asked to do for the project clearly spelled out. Otherwise, misunderstanding can occur as projects often grow above and beyond what was originally agreed upon. The client then may believe that the additional work falls under the scope of the agreement, without any additional costs. We recommend that you have great clarity in the agreement and are thorough listing out all tasks, the steps you are agreeing to do, the checkpoints, the sign-off processes, and the exact payment structure and timeline as well as all pertinent dates. This is not an all-inclusive list. It is only some of the items that typically are within business consulting agreements.

Confidentiality must also be addressed. Essentially, this means that you agree to keep information about your engagement, your project, and other elements of your work at the client site confidential from the rest of the world. You are there in confidence to do a particular job that may give you access to information that the rest of the world does not have. The confidentiality agreement will typically say you are duty bound not to share that information and that there can be legal repercussions if you do share that information.

Non-disclosure is basically the same idea. You will not be disclosing information that you are learning about the other party. You are promising to keep what should be confidential, confidential, and you will not to disclose that information with other people. We like to have dual confidentiality agreements in place that protect both parties so that your client does not share things they learn about you or from you without your permission. A dual confidentiality agreement will protect both parties so that you can confidently proceed in the course of your agreement and build a relationship on trust. This way both you and the client can provide whatever information is required so that you can get the job done to the best of your ability and achieve your project goals.

If you have employees or independent contractors working for you, then you will also want to have confidentiality and non-disclosure agreements in place with them so that your intellectual property is protected, and they will not share your proprietary information or client information with the rest of the world. Now remember, a contractor that you hire is basically a free agent who can work for themselves or for other people. They may be working with you for a specific project, and maybe multiple specific projects, but they are not an employee. They are bound by different protections that you normally have for employees of your company. It is absolutely necessary that you protect your intellectual property and that your clients are protected through the extension of the contracts that you have with your contractors. Just be certain, with an attorney's help, that everything is tight up and down this line, from the client, to you, to your contractors. Have contracts in place to assure that everyone is protected and safe.

Again, safety and trust is created with a simple agreement with any independent contractors and with your clients that defines your relationship, and then other task orders or statements of work can be defined for each independent project that are subordinate to that first agreement, recognizing that they are parts of that initial agreement which you both have signed. This simple, one- or two-page agreement can establish that your company has a relationship with the client and that all elements of the project work will be defined on subsequent "task orders," which reference the original agreement. Be certain that you make very clear the linkage of the relationship and that you and your company are not employees of your client's company. Also ensure that every piece of work has its own task order that defines the details of who is doing what, what the deliverables are, and what the fees are. Never forget the financial consideration of money and exchange for value delivered.

You may have one task order with a client or you may have multiple task orders with the same client over and over and over again for each additional piece of work that you do over the years. Task orders are based on your personal preference so determine how you want to handle them.

This task order process we are recommending acts as an extension of your first agreement, if you and the client choose to extend the engagement beyond the initial plan period for that first agreement. As an example, if you have a day rate that you define, you can say that after such and such a date, the parties agree to continue on with the day rate as long as you are doing the same type of work at the same rate, until the parties choose to cancel. We use contracts like these in our businesses, many that were signed a few years ago and we are still doing the same basic type of work—and have not had to have a new contract written as a result.

In the consulting business, projects seem to have a life of their own once begun, so, the signed contract protects you, and your client, and the relationship that you could have for years to come.

**Remember, for bonus resources
related to this chapter, go to:**

www.TheUltimateGamePlanBook.com/resources

CHAPTER 19

• • • • • • •

WHAT IS THE CORRECT LEGAL STRUCTURE FOR MY COMPANY?

IN THIS CHAPTER, WE WILL review what you need to know to set up your consulting business. Even if you're already an established business consultant, give this chapter a fast read to check that you have everything in place. There's a chance that you might get some important insight that will save you headaches down the road.

For new business consultants, read this chapter carefully! This information is important because you are not playing with an interesting hobby, but are launching a company that will help business leaders, may employ people who join your team, and has its own legal responsibilities. The last thing we would want for you is to make some avoidable mistakes as you set up your company the wrong way.

To keep out of trouble, take a lot of notes as you read this chapter. With that in mind, here's what this chapter is and what it is isn't. This chapter is a helpful guide to list out topics that you need to learn about. It is based on our current understanding given our experiences in setting up our own companies and helping our clients set up theirs. This chapter is *not* legal or financial advice. You need to go to your professional legal, tax, financial, and other advisors to confirm the best path for you. This chapter will be useful to speed your learning curve and queue up questions that will make your time with advisors more effective and beneficial.

With this introduction in mind, jump into this chapter with an open mind and learn everything you can so you can form your business with confidence. There's a lot of content in here—if you have questions, write them down in the margin and flag the pages so you can easily come back to this chapter as a resource.

Remember, this is an exciting time for you. Have fun!

COMMON BUSINESS STRUCTURES

When you form your business, the first thing you have to consider is what legal structure is best for you. There are many types of business structures for you to consider. The popular ones are:

* Sole Proprietor
* Partnership
* Corporation (C Corp or S Corp)
* Limited Liability Company
* Limited Liability Partnership

Here's a quick description of each so you can get an idea of the differences. Reviewing this content is an important first step of your research as you decide which business structure is best for you. It is also important for you to seek advice from your attorney, insurance provider, CPA, and financial advisor to discuss the legal and tax implications of these different choices so that you can select the one that is the best alternative for you. Yes, we know we said that already. We will probably say it again because it's important—you need to consult with your team of advisors. If you don't yet have advisors, read the chapter so that you'll know what best to be asking as you look to hire them.

In every type of company listed here, you will also want to understand the different insurance options to protect your company and your personal assets. Your company structure will provide one level of protection. Your insurance policies will provide additional protection. Make sure you recognize where your gaps reside and discuss your risks with your insurance agent to make sure you're covered.

SOLE PROPRIETORSHIP

In a sole proprietorship, you are the only person within your business. Legally, there is no distinction between you and your business. That means that your personal assets are not protected as they might be with a different business structure. While this is an easy way to start your business, there is also legal exposure for you as the business owner. If you choose this route, be sure to understand the risks and speak to your insurance carrier about the types and levels of insurance you could have for additional protection.

If you are a one-person consulting company, this may be a good option for you to consider so that you can get started right away with your consulting business. It is quick and easy, and may bridge the gap in time between you starting today and when you choose an alternative business structure at some point in the future. Just know that if your business is sued, your personal assets are not separate or protected. This is where you hear horror stories of someone who thought their business was a separate entity, was sued, and lost their house, their car, and their dog. There's probably a country song written about this scenario. If you are okay with this level of risk, go for it. We want to make sure you're fully aware as you make your decisions.

PARTNERSHIP

In a partnership, two or more individuals each have a share of the business. Each partner contributes to all aspects of the business, including money, property, labor, or ideas. In return, each partner shares in the profits and losses of the business.

If you have more than one owner in your business consulting company, then a partnership is a consideration. If you go this route, it is critical for you to be clear about roles and responsibilities for each of the partners and to spell them out in proper legal agreements. Just as many married couples who were once in love find themselves dividing their marital assets (including the same house, car, and dog we mentioned above!), business partners sometimes have their own divorce and split up. Your roles and responsibilities need to be more than handshakes to keep you safe.

CORPORATION (C CORP OR S CORP)

Corporations are generally perceived to be larger businesses, such as those that make up the Fortune 500. The definition of a *corporation* from Merriam Webster is *"a large business or organization that under the law has the rights and duties of an individual and follows a specific purpose."* You might notice this definition implies larger companies, although there are exceptions, such as business consulting services.

C CORP

Most of the corporations you know of, such as Walmart, ExxonMobil, or Apple are considered C Corps, which is a classification the corporation makes when it is formed that designates the type of business and tax structure it follows. A C Corp is taxed as its own business entity, and then the owners are also taxed on the proceeds from the business they collect.

S CORP

A smaller business could choose to designate itself as a Corporation, Subclass S, also known as an S Corp. There are advantages for a small business to become an S Corp rather than a C Corp, including that the net income from the company passes through to the owner's individual tax returns for the purposes of paying taxes on the business. There are other tax differences when you compare the S Corp to other possible structures that you will want to discuss with your tax advisors.

If you are a small consulting company, you might choose to become an S Corporation, even if you are a one-person company. While you could opt to form a C Corp as a small business, this is not very common.

LIMITED LIABILITY COMPANY (LLC)

The LLC is a common business structure in today's world. It offers flexibility to you, the business owner, as well as simplicity in setting up your business. If you are a "Single-Member LLC" you can elect to be taxed as a sole proprietorship, and if you have multiple members, you could be taxed as a partnership or an S Corp, depending on your elections when you register your company. This can get complicated quickly if you don't have guidance, so be sure to ask your legal and tax advisors about your choices.

Many owners of smaller consulting companies select the Limited Liability Company because they desire the simplicity and flexibility. The net income flows directly to the owner's personal tax returns, and they still enjoy some protection of their personal assets.

LIMITED LIABILITY PARTNERSHIP (LLP)

In this business structure, there is more than one partner. The good news is one partner is not responsible or liable for another partner's misconduct or negligence. Like the LLC, the business structure has some elements of standard partnerships and of corporations to offer protection.

Many law firms use the LLP structure. If you have multiple partners in your firm, you might look into the LLP as an option for you.

You might have specific requirements depending on the business structure you form for your company. Know what those requirements are, and work with your advisor team to make sure you have everything you need. It is much easier to have these systems and processes working correctly from the beginning so that you can have ongoing confidence with your monthly reports that everything is in place. This is much better than a mad scramble at the end of the year to try to pull everything together for your CPA.

FILING YOUR BUSINESS

Once you know the business structure that is right for your company, you need to file the required paperwork in order to make your company official. There are a number of elements, including your company name, your business structure, and your tax election. For each of these, there are specific forms and paperwork that must be completed and filed with your state government. For those of you who are setting up your consulting company outside of the United States, check the local laws to understand the process in your country.

WHERE YOU CHOOSE TO FORM YOUR BUSINESS

The next decision for you is where you want to form your business. Each state within the United States has its own Secretary of State offices where all company information is filed. Most of the time, you will choose the state in which you reside. However, there could be other reasons you may pick another state. For example, what if you have a business partner that lives in a different state? Which state will you file your company in? It's possible that the tax laws or other business laws are different, and you will want to know which is more favorable for your company.

Nevada has some very convincing reasons for forming your business there. Nevada's laws give more protection and support to you as a small business owner. Delaware is an attractive state for large corporations to do business because of their tax laws, and many large companies have their headquarters there.

YOUR BUSINESS NAME

We recommend you don't spend a lot of money or time building your business brand until you know that your name is properly registered and protected, under the correct business entity. This will allow you to be confident that someone won't later sue you, demanding that you cease and desist using the name you've grown into your thriving company. That would be hugely disruptive!

You will need to check to see if your desired name for your company is available. This is important because someone else might already have your preferred name, which may prevent you from using that name. If you think about company names that have become huge brands, such as Coca-Cola, you may want to trademark the name of your company. The U.S. Patent and Trademark Office's has a trademark search tool that would come in handy, not only if you were thinking of trademarking, but also when choosing a name. And if you choose to pursue trademarking your business name, you will want the assistance of a business attorney who understands intellectual property laws.

Your name should communicate the purpose of your business and the products and services that you provide. Remember, people get an initial read on your company and make a first impression based on your company name. With this in mind, it's less important to come up with a cute name and more important to think about brand identity as you select your name. See if you can come up with a name that creatively includes your product or service or, even better, how your clients will feel when they work with you.

For example, the name of Pete's consulting company includes the first syllable of his last name, Win. Of course, Win also implies "winning" and that is what his consulting company is helping his clients to do—win the game they are playing. Terri's company, Heartrepreneur™ gives the actual benefit of working with her company—becoming more engaged with heart in business. We know consultants who have named their companies with some attributes of something personal to them, such as the postal code for the university they attended in England, or the names of their children. This is not wrong to do, so don't misunderstand what we are suggesting. Just know that there may be a better alternative name for your company than one named for your favorite pet.

So if your name is John Smith or Mary Jones, or Sally Simpson and you don't bother to register the name of your company then it is *you* that the state and federal governments will look at if anything is not correct.

Your correct legal name is required on all your forms and applications. You'll need this for obtaining your Taxpayer Identification Number (TIN), for opening a bank account, and for providing a W-9 to clients who choose to do business with you.

Want to lease a car under your company's name? You'd better have all your paperwork in order otherwise you won't get anyone to lease you a car. Want a business line of credit? Same advice: get your paperwork completed correctly!

No matter which state within which you decide to set up your company, the process of confirming that your name is available and then registering your business name is relatively straightforward. It is also important to get this process right, so get support from an attorney's office to make sure you're processing the paperwork correctly.

LEGAL NAME VERSUS "DOING BUSINESS AS" (DBA)

Remember, unless you define otherwise by filing the paperwork to form your company as something other than a sole proprietorship and register that name with the state, the legal default is that *you*, the owner, are liable for that business.

The DBA is a fictitious name that you want to use that is not exactly the same as your official legal name. There is a process of filing the DBA so that you can have permission to use that name.

For example, our official legal name is the Business Coach and Consultant Institute, LLC. We set that up knowing that there is a large number of business coaches who could learn consulting skills and extend their business reach to help more clients, so we included "Coach" as part of the name. Once we got rolling in creating live workshops and mentoring consultants in our mastermind programs, we realized that that name was quite a mouthful. We shortened the name in practice to the Business Consultant Institute, which is much easier to say. But that's a fictitious name—we didn't have a business filed by that name, so instead it is considered a DBA.

Check with your advisors, as not all states require you to register a fictitious name as DBA.

AFTER YOUR NAME IS APPROVED...

The Secretary of State will notify you that your company name is approved. When you receive your notification, get a high-five from a close friend. However, before you fully celebrate your new business though, there's a little more work to do before you're official. You will need to get a federal tax identification number, which is like a social security number for businesses. This is also called a Taxpayer Identification Number (TIN) or Employer Identification Number (EIN). The same way you need to have your social security number to open a bank account, get a car loan, or access other certain information, your business will require your TIN/EIN for the same types of activity.

Applying for your TIN/EIN is easy. You can do it online through your Secretary of State website. It might take one to two weeks through normal processing, but you might be able to get one instantly for an expedited fee. If you're in a hurry to get your TIN/EIN to set up an operating account at the bank, you can get the number over the phone.

Your bank will require the legal name and TIN/EIN to set up your account. You will want to have a primary bank account where you'll deposit your revenue and then use that money to pay your accounts payables. You might choose to hire a book-keeper or office manager to take care of these tasks so that you can focus on getting paying clients and delivering the reve-nue-producing work that generates cash flow for your business, or you can manage these activities yourself for a while until your volume picks up.

INSURANCE FOR YOUR BUSINESS TO CONSIDER

Another important consideration is insurance. Depending on the type of business structure you selected, you will have differ-ent levels of exposure that you will want to cover with insur-ance. Additionally, different aspects of how you do business and serve clients will dictate different insurance needs.

If you have employees, the law requires that you have workers compensation insurance. General liability insurance is best if you have a building where employees, suppliers, contractors, or customers/clients come to work or visit. Imagine the FedEx delivery guy trips on your carpet, twists his ankle and needs medical attention. Their insurance carrier might sue you. You can see why it is so important for you to have your personal assets protected with your business structure and general liability insurance to cover the medical bill.

Another type of insurance you might consider is professional liability insurance. When you are offering advice to a company or client that is going to cause them to make some big decisions, you want to be protected if something goes wrong with their results. They could succeed or fail based on a number of factors such as their ability to execute your recommendations, along with the soundness of your recommendations and advice. What if their results got worse and they want to blame you? Your professional liability policy is designed to protect you.

Your clients may also require you to have certain levels of insurance in place in order for them to even sign a contract with you. For example, we've had clients who have required our respective consulting businesses to carry $1 million of coverage of professional liability insurance. They also require general liability and sometimes want to be listed as an additional insured on our personal automotive insurance. This sounds crazy, but they're protecting themselves, too.

While these situations are not likely, we want you to be aware that it is possible your clients will make these requests. You might choose to wait on getting some of these insurances until a client requires them of you, because it is an added expense for your business—we get it! Yet, we do strongly suggest you get professional advice to make sure you have enough protection for your business. Review your contracts and insurance coverage with your attorney, CPA, and insurance and other advisors to figure out the right level of protection for you.

OTHER IMPORTANT ELEMENTS

Here are some other things to think about as you launch your consulting business: your office location, phone system, email address, website, your letterhead on proposals or invoices, and business cards. Each of these is a deliberate decision. Think through the image that you want to portray to your clients. As we discussed above, these decisions might also factor into your needs for business insurance.

Make sure you have a website domain that is consistent with your business name for the services you provide. And do not, we repeat, *not* have an e-mail address with @Yahoo or @Gmail as the domain. Your email is best tied to your website domain to appear professional rather than look like a start-up that does not have its act together.

Consider getting a logo done that professionally represents each of your businesses. You can hire a local graphics person or does someone online from a service like Fiverr^R or Upwork^{TM} where people will do quality work inexpensively. You can even have that same graphics person create templates for your business letterhead for your proposals and invoices.

As for business equipment, you will need a laptop computer, a smartphone, an Internet connection, and an all-in-one printer that connects to your wireless so you can print, scan, and possibly fax documents. That is about all you are required to get start-ed. As you grow, you can decide if you want to have a landline phone in an office location. You could get a nice headset for your phone and a USB headset for your computer so you can easily do Skype calls or webinars. You might add equipment such as a projector if you do a lot of public workshops, but this is prob-ably not necessary for client work because most clients have projectors on location. Terri invested in a portable sound system because of all the public speaking and workshops that she has done over the years, which saved her from renting the expensive sound system at the hotel, but again that is an advanced decision for you to *make after* you have many of the other elements of your business in place. You can invest in flip charts and mark-ers as these will come in handy in many situations. Beyond that, there's very little you need so stop thinking you have to acquire all these other things before you get started—it's time to act now. You have all you need!

YOUR SMALL BUSINESS ADMINISTRATION AND INTERNAL REVENUE SERVICE RESOURCES

The purpose of this section is to raise your awareness about the multiple elements of launching your business to get you started. Many of your initial questions can be answered by the resources provided by the U.S. Small Business Administration. Look at the sba.gov site for a quick set of answers to your fre-quently asked questions. They will help you get a little smart-er before you discuss your options with your attorney, CPA, or other advisors. For example, did you know that your federal tax liability will be different depending on what type of business entity you selected? The SBA website will help you understand the different types of business taxes that you'll have to pay.

The federal government requires four types of business taxes: income taxes, self-employment tax, employment tax if you have employees, and excise taxes depending on the type of products and services you provide. You need to make regular, estimated tax payments to the government (not just before April 15th at the end of the tax season). IRS.gov is a useful resource to help you find answers, or at least conduct your first level of research before you arrange a meeting with your professional advisors.

RECORD KEEPING

Regardless of what type of an entity you decide to form, you need to have excellent systems and processes in place such as record keeping. You will also want to have visibility to your revenues, costs, and cash flow as well as mechanisms to keep costs down and cash flow high. Track your conversations with prospects, including what materials you send them to get them excited about working with you. Tracking what works well will simplify future marketing endeavors.

**Remember, for bonus resources
related to this chapter, go to:**

www.TheUltimateGamePlanBook.com/resources

SECTION VIII

• • • • • • •

YOUR NEXT ACTIONS

Now that you've read and digested most of this book, we want to make sure you're thinking about what actions to take. Yes, it's wise to re-read your notes, skim the chapters and decide how to put the advice and strategies to use. In addition, we want you to go a little further with these two very important exercises described in this section.

In Chapter 20, you will get clear about what you stand for and develop the guiding principles for your consulting company. Read this carefully, because there is more here than you might expect.

In Chapter 21, we share an extremely powerful success exercise that can accelerate you achieving your business goals and beyond. Take it seriously and enjoy your results.

CHAPTER 20

• • • • • • •

DEVELOP YOUR GUIDING PRINCIPLES

WE WANT YOU TO MAKE A commitment to your clients, your team, and yourself about what your company stands for. We want you to declare what's important to you, and then live according to those principles.

We call these *Guiding Principles*, but broadly recognize these to represent your Purpose, Vision, Mission, Values, or other names you give to the list of things that are important to you. Let's agree to not get caught up in the definition similarities and differences among these different terms. The most important thing is to know what principles are most important to you and your business, why they are important, and then to behave in alignment with those principles.

Give some thought for a few moments to who you are, why you're here on the planet, and how you want to see the world working as if everything were perfect. Consider your bigger reason for starting your consulting business. Sure, you want to earn buckets of money to fund your kids' college tuition payments or the extra time off that your business will enable for you... but *why else?* What is your bigger cause? What do you want to create in the world by growing your consulting company?

We know that at this stage of the book, you're already really excited about how you can grow your consulting business. You might already have taken notes about possible clients you want to work with. Maybe you have begun to list out the attributes of your Perfect Client and begun to list of who you would love to work with as their consultant. So why are these clients on your list? What makes them perfect for you?

Go further in your introspective exercise here and picture the difference you're able to make for them. Now identify why that's important to you.

Are you taking this seriously? If so, you're starting to see how you can really make a difference in this world. This isn't simply by creating millions of dollars of value for your clients so they can become more profitable, which of course will create a nice, successful business for you. Envision beyond the economics. How are you positively impacting people's lives? How are you making a difference for the business leaders and team members? What about for the people on your team? What about for your family and for yourself?

Now you're getting somewhere!

The reason we are so passionate about this is that you have an opportunity to become a leader in the consulting industry. No, we don't mean we expect that your annual revenue will compete with the biggest or most prestigious firms like McKinsey and Company, Accenture, Bain Consulting, or Boston Consulting Group. We do fully expect that you will become a leader in how you behave, what motivates you, and the impact you have in the world.

Outside the Fortune 500, most businesses do not hire these large, prestigious firms—they hire consultants like you. It is you and your peers that collectively shape how clients think about consultants, and we all have a responsibility to hold each other accountable to a higher standard of excellence.

RAISE THE BAR FOR ALL CONSULTANTS

During our consulting careers, we have both encountered clients who have had poor experiences with consultants in the past, and are now reluctant to hire any consultants no matter how great the consulting company might be or how dire the client's need is. They simply refuse to do it.

The reality is that there are some consulting companies out there that do a poor job. This is both good and bad news for you.

So first the good news. As you follow the advice and strategies we are sharing in this book, you will become an elite consultant—with skills and abilities to create exceptionally impressive results and deliver enormous impact for your clients. They will love you, tell their peers about your stellar performance, and your business will skyrocket! Your ability to form great relationships and deliver value to your clients will become a differentiator for you, especially compared to these other poor-performing consultants.

Unfortunately, the fact that there are inferior consultants out there will actually hurt you. Think of this: because of other consultants who possess inadequate skills, a deficiency in their experience, motivations that put themselves first before their clients, or simply are not able to deliver satisfactory results, business leaders form a negative opinion about consultants in general. Your potential clients might become shy about hiring *any* consultant because of their undesirable experiences with "poor" consultants. This is discouraging for you because you didn't do anything to deserve that black mark against you, and yet a client who could benefit from your help might not consider hiring you.

It is for these reasons that it is imperative that we *all* help create an amazing set of experiences for our clients. The industry is expanding and will continue to grow, and there will be plenty of pie for us all if can continue to demonstrate tremendous value. Make this a business priority for you and part of your guiding principles.

THE GUIDING PRINCIPLES OF THE BUSINESS CONSULTANT INSTITUTE

We are not asking you to become something that you are not, and we are not asking you to do anything that we are not also willing to do. We emphatically believe in our guiding principles, and want you to create principles for yourself, as well.

We both believe that walking our talk and living within our values contributes greatly to our success. We are what you see. We stand firm in our commitment to give the highest value to our clients, engage in continuous growth, and continually raise the bar on our performance.

Integrity is the center point on all of our activities. Without integrity, we'd all be consultants viewed like snake oil salesmen standing on a street corner pushing our products—clients will not trust us! Integrity is woven into every engagement, every presentation—and it's even in our mission statement—"to help consultants maximize their impact for their clients, while operating in the highest integrity, which then creates an abundance of clients and income for consultants."

And as an industry we have a responsibility to act with integrity at all times. Many of your clients—or prospects—have lost faith in our industry because of bad experience with consultants who are merely out to make a buck—and lack the commitment to actually help the clients by adding the highest value possible during engagements.

To be truthful, there are a lot of bad consultants who don't *know* they are bad. They only have a couple of tools and that's how they approach *all* client problems. They subscribe to the "take this pill, and call me in the morning approach" of masking symptoms rather than creating solutions that are sustainable.

So here are the principles by which we live:

1. Trust that our knowledge and experience will help someone solve problems.

2. Align ourselves with our mission and values with complete clarity.

3. Courageously be ourselves at all times.

4. Be principle based, not tool based, as this delivers better client impact.

5. Focus on building long-term relationships.

6. Present ourselves to the world as a way to *attract* to us the right people to work with and help in their journeys.

7. Engage in continual self-improvement—both personally and professionally so that we can offer our clients the very best of who we can be.

8. Raise the bar even higher than we ever imagined possible to continue to challenge ourselves and to make a difference in our world.

So remember, to be a successful consultant and make the most meaningful impact on your clients, and possibly the world—Live in high integrity, and stay in high integrity. You can make a difference when you stay true to your Guiding Principles.

Remember, for bonus resources
related to this chapter, go to:

www.TheUltimateGamePlanBook.com/resources

CHAPTER 21

* * * * * * *

DESCRIBE YOUR FUTURE

YOUR NEXT ACTION IS QUITE fun and energizing. We want you to describe your consulting business in the future. No matter where you are today, from just getting started to having a decade of solid experience, we want you to go five or ten years further into the future and imagine what your consulting will look like.

Here we are engaging some of the science of success principles and tools, where visualization is a powerful tool to provide direction to your unconscious mind of what you desire your reality to look like.

HOW VISUALIZATION WORKS

Your brain has multiple functions, including running all the parts of your mind and body on autopilot. Despite your wishes, your unconscious mind will actually work harder to keep you right where you are than it will to move you into some new unknown territory. Why? It wants to protect you and keep you safe. Building a consulting business, going out into the wild to get clients, asking for a new contract, etc.— this is all new territory that your unconscious mind could decide is just a bit too far outside your comfort zone for it to endorse your desires and support your journey.

Until, that is, you convince it that you're serious and you really do want to move into this new unfamiliar world of running your massively successful consulting business.

This is where your persistence and clarity come into play. When you have tremendous focus about your goals, knowing with full emotional excitement that achieving your goals is simply a foregone conclusion, and that you can fully envision what success looks, feels, tastes, smells, and sounds like—then you can begin to have your unconscious mind pay attention to you. It appreciates you and how clear you are.

Now for persistence, you need daily reminders (in fact, multiple times each day is best) of what your future looks like after you have achieved the full level of success you desire. The exercise is generically called visualizing, but it could include activities beyond the images you daydream about that live solely in your mind. You could also build a physical visual portfolio of images and words that represent the level of success you desire.

For example, if you have a goal to go on a vacation to Paris, you might print an image of the Eiffel Tour and hang it on the wall in your office or upload it to be part of your screen saver. Or, if you want to build a consulting firm that has ten employees, imagine a team photo in the office space you have. Find an image of something that represents the office space and team members you desire to help anchor your imagery.

Lastly, your level of belief will either shut you down or accelerate your achievements. If you have an unconscious little voice encouraging you, you will unknowingly make decisions that will bring you toward your success more quickly as you recognize the nearly invisible opportunities that present themselves to you. If your little voice suggests you are not worthy, then similarly it will ensure you stay right where you are by ignoring the opportunities that come along.

Your brain is on autopilot for the majority of all its functions. Don't believe us? Did you tell your brain to beat your heart or your lungs to take a breath? What about your drive home—Do you remember deciding your route yesterday? There are way too many inputs for your brain to concern you with. It just takes over on your behalf, delivering you the existence it thinks you want.

The part of your brain called the Reticular Activating System (RAS) has the job of the filter to decide what inputs come into your awareness. Here is how it works. You just purchased a new grey Jeep Grand Cherokee and you suddenly notice tons of other grey Jeep Grand Cherokees on the road (that were always there but you didn't notice them before). If you can direct your brain to pay attention to specific things for you—like your goals—then you will start to notice ways to achieve them, too.

Visualizing the future you want for yourself and your business is a critical step in helping to teach your unconscious mind that you are serious about creating this outcome. In fact, you want to engage your brain's help to make this your reality as quickly as possible. Deeply believe that you deserve the level of success you describe. Reinforce this belief by visualizing the details of your success every day, and you will indeed get there more quickly.

YOUR EXERCISE

Imagine that you have successfully implemented the strategies we describe in this book. Pretend that for any challenge you encountered along the way, we were there to support you and answer your questions. You picked up this book and magically flipped to the pages that you need to answer your questions. Or, fantasize about having access to ask us specific questions directly to get our help, personally.

With all this support and the foregone conclusion that you will achieve whatever you wish, what level of success do you desire? Describe:

* your success in terms of your revenue, and how much money you make

* the attributes of your perfect client, and write down how many clients you have

* what your engagements look like and the terms of the contracts you sign—are you working with the same client for multiple years with a big team of resources, or are you working with multiple clients for shorter engagements

* your team members, and how many people are on your team

* your office and work environment

* every other attribute of your life that your success has enabled, including the house you live in, the cars you drive, the vacations you take, and anything else you desire

This is fully and completely your future to design any way you'd like, without restrictions. The strategies we have taught you will take you there—now all you have to do is implement them.

**Remember, for bonus resources
related to this chapter, go to:**

www.TheUltimateGamePlanBook.com/resources

CONCLUSION

• • • • • • •

OUR GOAL IN WRITING THIS BOOK was to help you, as a business consultant, to learn how to *build* a successful consulting business or to *improve* your already successful consulting business. Our intention was to show you what worked well in our consulting businesses and to share what we have mentored our mastermind clients to do in their businesses that have made them successful consultants, as well. Through learning from our successes, we want you to massively increase your success in your consulting business.

We know that our mastermind clients love the information we shared with you in this book. They tell us that with the information we provide, we have taken away a lot of the marketing stress and answered their questions about how to have successful consulting engagements—and a revenue stream that is reliable.

Now that you have completed the book, we hope you can see how an ideal consulting business runs and how to make your business very profitable. We want you to create your business to be low stress. We know you can have the freedom in your business that you deserve—and you will when you implement the systems and solutions in this book.

As we have been mentoring clients at Business Consultant Institute, and they've implemented the tips and information in this book, we hear that they feel a lot less overwhelmed when starting or growing their consulting businesses. Both of us want for you, just like our mastermind clients, to have a lot more enjoyment in your consulting business. And if you're happily engaged in your business, that will have a ripple effect on your clients. We know that happier clients are those clients who stay long term and even refer business.

We're guessing that you read this book because you have the desire to build a successful consulting business. Our job, as mentors and authors, was to show you exactly how to do this. We laid out the game plan for you and now all you need to do is run with the ball. And when you do, you will get the kind of results that you want with your clients, as well as have the income you desire by constantly having a stream of clients coming to you—when you take *action*.

COMMIT TO FIVE STRATEGIES

In this book, we have given you all the tools you need to take the necessary actions and get that ball rolling! If you are brand new to consulting and do not yet have any clients, then right now is the time for you to figure out how to position yourself to the market and identify your ideal first client. Get the picture of your ideal client, and then select the companies that you would like to work with. If you are an existing consulting company and want to grow your business, flip through the paragraphs about retaining clients, adding services, cross selling, upselling and look for our ideas that can literally double your business.

No matter where you currently are in your consulting business, we suggest you pick out only five strategies from the book and commit to fully implementing those five in the next three months. As our mentoring clients have demonstrated, just five strategies will make a world of difference to your income and your long-term consulting success.

If you want additional resources, tools, mentoring, or coaching go over to: www.BusinessConsultantInstitute.com/ultimate-gameplanresources

If you want to be considered for our mastermind or individual mentoring, email us at info@businessconsultantinstitute.com.

If you are interested in attending, one of our live programs visit: www.businessconsultantevent.com.

Finally, we want to hear from *you* and about your success with this book. Pay a visit to Amazon if you enjoyed the book and write a review about what parts of the book resonated with you and share your review with others. Think of two other people who might enjoy the book. Get one for a friend or colleague and another for someone you want to make amends with. And be certain to email us at info@businessconsultantinstitute.com to tell us your story.

It is our pleasure to serve other business consultants, and it is our joy to watch consultants grow and prosper with our help.

We wish you the very best of luck as you now *Power Up Your Consulting Business* and skyrocket your revenues!

Terri Levine and Pete Winiarski

WE ARE HERE FOR YOU

* * * * * * *

BY NOW, YOU KNOW WHO we are, that we have a tremendous track record of success, and how we help and serve business consultants.

As you have been reading this book, have you wondered what it would be like to access us and ask us questions?

Have you imagined getting our help to skyrocket the results in your consulting business?

Are you open to having us nurture you and take you under our wings, like we have done and are doing for so many other business consultants?

Take a moment and think what it might be like to have our help.

To show you the possibilities, here are a few words from our clients:

"Following their strategies, I have literally doubled my business in the first six months. With the specific approaches of interacting with past clients, relationships that were dormant for years have been rekindled, resulting in engagements all over the world."

Maryanne Ross, President, Mental Apparel

"Right away I was able to knock out some phenomenal results. Just this week we inked a deal where I have $50,000 worth of business coming in. So Terri & Pete, thanks a lot! It's working already!"

Dave Garrison, President, Garrison Productivity Solutions

"Participating in the Business Consultants Institute summits and mastermind with Terri and Pete helped to rapidly redefine, reinvent and ramp up my consultancy to higher levels. Through a combination of subtle shifts in mindset and methodology— and specific insights and interventions—I was able to easily handle challenges, leverage opportunity, incubate a new body of work with greater impact and revenue, and quickly acquire several new ideal clients."

Robert Merlin Davis, creator of The Merlin Method

"Pete has the incredible deep background in consulting and Terri is a marketing mastermind. Put those two together and it's a great combination."

David Tweedt, President, Win Consulting

"I have gotten value, value, value! I can say at least ten times the amount of money I invested I have gotten it back... $100,000 in less than 9 months and there is still more left!"

Ilka Chavez, President, Corporate Gold, LLC

WHAT'S NEXT

We've shared our knowledge, personal stories, experiences, learnings, and given you some deep insight into becoming a very successful business consultant. We put a great deal of time, energy and focus into creating this book so it would be your business consulting "bible."

We also know that what is missing is the actual experience of working with us and having us mentor you on every area and topic covered in this book, plus tons more advanced consulting topics we didn't have time to capture for this book.

This book is literally the tip of the iceberg.

Remember, we only succeed when our clients succeed and when you learn more, you earn more. We are therefore totally committed to teaching you what we know works so that you can knock it out of the park!

If you are ready to create your consulting business, take your existing consulting business to the next level, or even are thinking about selling your consulting business, then we are the right business mentors for you.

We know that the most successful people take action. They don't sit on an idea, or sleep on it, or consult the stars about it.

If you are serious about being successful with your consulting business, then go to http://www.businessconsultantinstitute.com/apply and apply for a profit session with us.

There is no obligation and no strings attached. We can get to know each other, share some tools, tips, and strategies with you, and then see if there is a fit for us to mentor you.

Take the next step right now:

http://businessconsultantinstitute.com/apply

ABOUT THE AUTHORS

. . . .

TERRI LEVINE

Terri Levine is the bestselling author of almost a dozen books and the Chief Heartrepreneur™ at http://www.heartrepreneur.com, and is known as the business-mentoring expert with heart. Her latest book, *Turbocharge How to Transform Your Business As A Heartrepreneur™* has become an overnight success. (https://goo.gl/pdkFyV)

Terri was named one of the top ten coaching gurus in the world by www.coachinggurus.net and the top female coach in the world. She has received recognition from every major coaching organization and association, has been assisting businesses worldwide with creating the right inner mindset and outer actions for business growth. Terri has been mentoring business leaders and team members for over three decades and helped over five thousand business owners to go from ordinary to extraordinary while having the life of their dreams, doing the work they love, loving the work they do, and being financially secure too!

As a keynote speaker, Terri has inspired hundreds of thousands of people through her high-content, memorable, and motivational speeches. She has been featured in the media on platforms such as ABC, NBC, MSNBC, CNBC, *Fortune, Forbes, Shape, Self, The New York Times*, the BBC, and in more than fifteen hundred publications. Her radio show, *The Terri Levine Show: Business Advice You Can Take to the Bank,* is downloaded by thousands of people from her iHeart Radio channel each month. http://www.iheart.com/show/209-The-Terri-Levine-Show/

Terri holds a PhD in clinical psychology, is a Master Certified Guerrilla Marketing Trainer and Coach, and is accredited by the American Association of Business Psychology. She is a Licensed Hidden Marketing Assets Consultant, she is managing director for Polka Dots Powerhouse, and a founding member of the Evolutionary Business Council where she also serves as a call leader, and the Philadelphia Ambassador for the organization. She is a mentor for StrongBrook Mentoring Network, and sits on the board of four nonprofit organizations.

She operates http://www.heartrepreneur.com, mentoring business owners to turbocharge their business to create more revenues and profits while learning to be Heartrepreneurs.

Terri is the co-founder of http://www.businessconsultantinstitute.com and https://www.businessconsultantevent.com, training business consultants to create super profitable consulting businesses.

Terri is also on the advisory board of several companies and dedicates time fundraising for the nonprofit foundation she founded, The Terri Levine Foundation for Children with RSD. (http://www.TerriLevinefoundationforchildrenwithRSD.org)

PETE WINIARSKI

Peter (Pete) D. Winiarski is highly sought after business consultant, speaker, media guest, and best-selling author. Pete is known as a business transformation expert and a goal achievement expert.

Having thirty years of experience in leadership roles, Pete leads his consulting company, Win Enterprises, LLC, to help business leaders transform their results with a team of resources who are experts in business transformation, process improvement using "Lean" principles, organization culture, leadership, and goal achievement.

His website, https://www.completebusinesstransformation. com, is an abundant resource for business leaders to help guide their business improvement for long-term and sustainable results.

Pete is the creator of the Win Holistic Transformation Model™, a complete approach for companies to experience lasting transformational change. He is also the co-creator of the Conscious Leadership Model, and teaches leaders how to maximize their effectiveness as leaders of others by first leading themselves.

Pete is the author of the #1 International Best Selling book *Act Now! A Daily Action Log for Achieving Your Goals in 90 Days* and is in process of publishing six other books on business transformation and consulting.

Pete has appeared as a business expert and a goal-achievement expert in multiple media outlets, including ABC, CBS, FOX, NBC, and Industry Week.

Pete has been trained and mentored by Jack Canfield, and is one of just a few people around the world to achieve "Certified Senior Trainer" status to deliver Jack's work.

Pete is the co-founder of the Business Consultant Institute, at http://www.businessconsultantinstitute.com and http://www.businessconsultantevent.com, which trains business consultants to create super profitable consulting businesses.

In his spare time, Pete coaches and plays baseball, enjoys live music, and supports whatever activities his wife and two sons are pursuing.